# WISDOM *and the* SENSES

*Also by Joan M. Erikson*


VITAL INVOLVEMENT IN OLD AGE
(with Erik H. Erikson and Helen Q. Kivnick, Ph.D.)

ACTIVITY, RECOVERY, GROWTH
THE COMMUNAL ROLE OF PLANNED ACTIVITIES
(with David and Joan Loveless)

SAINT FRANCIS AND HIS FOUR LADIES

THE UNIVERSAL BEAD

MĀTĀ NĪ PACHEDĪ:
THE TEMPLE CLOTH OF THE MOTHER GODDESS

# WISDOM
## *and the*
# SENSES

## *The Way of Creativity*

# JOAN  M.  ERIKSON

W · W · NORTON & COMPANY
*New York*  ·  *London*

First published as a Norton paperback 1991

Printed in the United States of America.

The text of this book is composed in Lino Walbaum,
with display type set in Lino Walbaum.
Composition and manufacturing by
the Maple-Vail Book Manufacturing Group.
Book design by Jacques Chazaud.
Color photographs by Jon M. Erikson.

Library of Congress Cataloging in Publication Data

Erikson, Joan M. (Joan Mowat)
Wisdom and the senses : the way of creativity / Joan M. Erikson.
p. cm.
Includes index.
1. Creative ability.  2. Wisdom.  3. Life cycle, Human.
4. Senses and sensation.  I. Title.
BF408.E75  1988
153.3′5—dc19  87–35312

ISBN-13: 978-0-393-30710-8
ISBN-10: 0-393-30710-7

W. W. Norton & Company, Inc.
500 Fifth Avenue, New York, N.Y. 10110
www.wwnorton.com

W. W. Norton & Company Ltd.
Castle House, 75/76 Wells Street, London W1T 3QT

5 6 7 8 9 0

This book is dedicated to

NINA PAYNE

poet, teacher, and friend

Nina Payne gave me the initial courage to undertake the writing of this book. Ilana Fortgang helped me with unstinting support to finish and send it off for publication. I am deeply grateful. As always, Erik's purview and approval provided unfailing impetus.

To all the good friends and co-workers who have left their imprint on this book I offer my heartfelt thanks. I hope sincerely that my inadequacies in presenting their contributions have not betrayed their trust; I am greatly in their debt.

Arden Parish and May Hipshman have devotedly typed and retyped this manuscript. I thank them warmly.

# Contents

# CONTENTS

# Introduction

Should you judge, on seeing the title of this book, that it is presumptuous to undertake to deal with these difficult and disparate topics in one short book, I would be in complete agreement. If I then admit to having also included considerable reflection on creativity and the human life cycle, that may be the end of our relationship, which I would deplore. But I have spent years living with and examining the relationship of the senses to the wisdom that is supposed to come to fruition in old age. The search has been an expansive one encompassing the life cycle and leading to a surprising conclusion.

For the most part we take the senses for granted and become aware of their fragility and limitations only when they begin to lose their acuity and "give out." Then we complain bitterly and rush off to buy hearing aids, glasses, improved teeth, and walking sticks.

Perhaps artists are the first to become aware of these depreciations since they depend so consistently on the acuity of their senses. In any case, to live creatively is a life-long goal for many who are not professional artists, and this "way" demands attention to keen perception.

Memorable sensory experiences are often fleeting but may for a period of time be stayed by creatively giving them form. The realization of such a "holding" is only possible by means of lawful processes and disciplined, attentive work. When the product is faithful to what our senses have taught us and what our informed imaginations have grasped, when it has been executed with integrity and conveys a universal truth, it may become genuine artistic expression. All the arts are governed by these standards and the products of each age stage can exemplify for that stage an appropriate level of accomplishment which remains fundamental to artistic integrity. Thus we use the term "creative activities" for the very young who are involved in art experiences and for those who have come late to such involvement, and save the word "art" for riper fruit. But all the ingredients are there in early vestiges from the beginning, and consistent involvement and time develop the product—the masterpiece.

Only in old age, I submit, does it become incontrovertibly clear that to grasp the meaning of our lives we need a deep understanding of human development and the epigenetic stages through which life inevitably takes us. Any child, adult, or aging person embarks on this journey whenever a creative project is undertaken. In this book three artists—a painter, a weaver, and a composer—describe for us, in their own words, their lives, experiences, and the satisfactions of their chosen calling.

Finally we focus our attention on wisdom: where to look for clarification and enlightenment in ancient records, holy writ, and artifacts; what archetypal figures have symbolized wisdom; the attributes of wise old men and women; and what we can learn from such sources about how to live. I shall be advocating creativity and the way of the artist throughout this presentation. It is a hard way of life in our technological world, where success is measured by economic standards and few aspirants achieve acclaim.

The schooling we offer our young does not consistently expose them to experience in the arts yet we feel free to judge whether individuals are or are not "talented." This is an august method of reaching such a conclusion. Too often only the "gifted" child is offered encouragement, opportunity, and support in artistic interests.

No one will deny the supreme accomplishment of the great work of art: the symphony, ballet, opera, poem, drama, monument, or painting. What we tend to deny is that these are the fruits and that without attention to the early growth of the plant there would be no harvest. One must emphasize, however, that there is an integrity and a perfection in the twig, the bud, and the blossom—a perfection appropriate to the stage of its development. Let us pursue this metaphor.

What we do deny in our culture is that in early development the tree itself must be afforded space and every kind of care in order to foster stagewise growth and final fruit. We seldom speak of gifted trees as we do of gifted individuals. Rather, we acclaim fine orchards and vineyards and vintages and accord respect to those that have provided the consistent cultivation and pruning. Such husbanding of all our creative potentialities could result in a great renaissance of art here and everywhere. How splendid that could be to allow every embryonic Shakespeare, Rodin, and O'Keeffe to develop his or her highest capacities, to have numerous Edisons, Curies, and Einsteins advancing our understanding of nature's forces without depleting them and also creating the beauty which lifts our spirits.

Even that, however, would not be the highest good. The most challenging goal would be for all human beings to regain and maintain vital growth by means of the development of acute senses that could monitor all relationships with the ecology of the earth in which we live and create. For our sensory understanding is what makes humankind one species with one universal language—the inborn language of all creativity, of all the crafts and the great arts. This is an old idea and yet ever new and increasingly meaningful.

> All things are implicated with one another, and the bond is holy: and there is hardly any thing unconnected with any other thing.
>
> (MARCUS AURELIUS, A.D. 180)

I have been reluctant to let this manuscript go. Each section seems inclined to grow and has been deprived, as yet, of full development. Perhaps a green thumb somewhere will feel challenged to nurture further growth.

# WISDOM *and the* SENSES

# 1

# Our Vital Resources:
# The Senses

Many years ago, William James wrote an essay entitled *On Vital Reserves.** In it he claims that we are all using only a very small portion of the energy and attention of which we are capable. This essay was widely read and quoted, since it presented a formidable challenge. The problem and the challenge still exist, indeed more urgently than before, and I would like to consider what the reasons may be for our lethargy—our dullness. I mean, of course, compared to what we might be—to what our potentials promise. How could we be more vitally alive?

What do our potentials promise, and when do they first become apparent? A discussion of beginnings must nec-

*William James, *On Vital Reserves.* New York: Henry Holt, 1922.

essarily focus on the human embryo cradled in its matrix of amniotic fluid in the womb.

One of the most recent frontiers of research in human development has been inquiry into the sensory response of the fetus. Let me offer a very brief summary of the motility and sensory receptivity of that fetus in "paradise." These are evoked responses, the earliest occurring at 7.5 weeks of gestation, the first being relatively undifferentiated.

Numerous reflex responses have been photographically documented somewhat later, but let us consider only two: hand movements and oral activity. These reflexes are stimulated by means of pinpoint touching of human embryos maintained in a heated water bath after premature birth.

Developmentally the grasp reflex progresses in the same sequence as that which is characteristic of the volitional development of grasp in the infant. The nose and mouth area elicits the first reflex activity and is considered the primary sensitivity, thus establishing the oral readiness of the newborn. The fetus drinks the amniotic fluid and sucks his thumb. All embryonic activity serves to keep the joints, tendons, and muscles operative, and fetal activity is connected with the inborn need to exercise and practice. All these induced reactions are exemplary of the capacity of the embryo to function at a very early stage of development.

Considerably more is now also known about the normal development of the senses in utero. Briefly, then, it has been verified that auditory functioning begins very early in the fetus and is demonstrable in a rudimentary way in the fifth month. This is certifiable by means of measuring the response in the rate of the heartbeat. Taste sensitivity is demonstrable earlier. The fetus can distinguish between the taste of amniotic fluid which has been sweetened and that which has not, measurably increasing consumption of the former. Since premature infants of 29 weeks are capable of opening their eyes, it is presumed that the human fetus also has this capacity, and it is plausible that reaction to varying light intensities is possible. "It appears that the uterus is an unexpectably varied source of sensory stimuli."*

Of course, there has long been the conviction that the mother's physical and emotional conditions influence the well-being of the fetus, and new methods of determining the heartbeat reactions of the fetus confirm these assumptions. The evidence would suggest that "the interaction between organism and environment begins in the prenatal phase" and that the "effects of the interaction are complex and prolonged."

With these new findings in mind, it is now not so surprising to read the recent report of developmental scientists on the response repertoire of the infant, stating that the newborn comes into the world with all *sensory modalities* functioning, their capabilities far exceeding what was suspected just a short time ago. Eye contact can be made by the infant with the mother even in the first days, and eyes can also follow objects and discriminate certain preferred colors. The newborn can discriminate the odor of his own mother and even choose to orient more in her direction. Taste perception is also amazingly acute at birth. As Lewis Lipsitt says:

> The newborn child is capable of experiencing a wide range of both appetitive and aversive stimulation; and
> . . . the infant's mechanisms for conveying to the world

*Pirkko L. Graves Phil, Ph.D., *The Functioning Fetus*, Vol. I, *Infancy and Early Childhood*. Washington, D.C.: Greenspan & Pollock/ NIMH, 1980.

his or her pleasure or displeasure with the nurturant or intrusive environment are already in place. In short, the newborn is ready to reciprocate. The environment acts on the infant, and the infant responds; but the responses of the infant are themselves stimuli capable of evoking responses in their caretakers. The baby may behave in such a way, through cuddling, for example, as to promote further cuddling, caressing, and eye contact.*

The human infant, then, arrives in the world ready for mutuality, for reciprocating relations, as the expert says, and is in fact already capable of learning. From birth on, the rate of development is astounding, and we are beginning to learn how important a role the environment and particularly the caring persons play in the acuteness of the evolving senses. Parents delight in observing this progress throughout the first year of their child's life, and their response stimulates the infant's pleasure in her own performance. Absence of such mutuality of stimulus or misuse of stimuli may retard development, sometimes resulting in permanent dysfunction.

Following birth the infant continues development at a phenomenal rate. If we consider only the continued development of the hand movements and the oral activity (mentioned earlier as accomplishments of the fetus), we are quite at a loss to adequately document in a brief way the extent of the progress apparent in the first and second years. Consider the constant grasping, from the earliest first instinctive efforts up to the controlled use of all fingers and especially the thumb. On the basis of the earliest sucking movements, an extraordinary develop-

*Lewis Lipsitt, *The Child in the World of Tomorrow: A Window into the Future.* Oxford/New York: Pergamon Press, 1979.

ment results in the ability to make sounds and form words, as well as to bite and chew. The almost constant delight in all bodily activity is thus a continuation of the need of the fetus to exercise and practice. A veritable drive toward mastery and competence distinguishes the relation of the child at this stage to both his musculature and the environment.

The development of the auditory capacities in these early years is equally astonishing. The attention necessary to acquire the fine tuning that is required to differentiate sound and tone and to understand the message is a great accomplishment. To be finally able to respond appropriately is another major achievement. Smelling and tasting become sensitively refined and even firmly idiosyncratic, all objects initially having been investigated by the discriminating mouth.

Perhaps the most important sensory apparatus to be aware of is the human infant's dependence on and consistent need for intimate closeness, for touching. The skin, which from head to foot relates us sensitively to the world in which we live, our matrix, is indeed our most consistently active and informing organ of sense. In a dark vacuum where only minimal sight, hearing, taste, smell, and muscle activity would be possible, the skin could still report something of the nature of the surroundings: dry, cold, wet, hot, soft, hard, pressure. This was at one time our total awareness of the nature of the sheltering womb. Now that we know how actively engaged the senses already are in utero, it is still thought provoking to realize how sensitively the skin reports its surroundings to the embryo.

When the infant has struggled its way into the world through the birth process, the adaptive demand on the skin is enormous. How that skin surface is first handled is of special significance. How it continues to be cared for, touched by caring fingers, and held in relation to human bodies is even more a matter of appropriate concern. A lifelong sensibility for physical intimacy and sensitivity to touch and perception is being formed and fostered. The consequence in our Western culture of having adapted to a technological, puritanical culture which underestimates our dependence on skin sensitivity should be gravely considered.

And what of the eyes? In utero, we are told, they are at most able to distinguish light from dark, as when, for example, in late pregnancy the mother's skin is drawn tight and thin over the abdomen, and the embryo is exposed to sunlight. At birth the eyes open, sometimes seemingly quite reluctantly in the glare of strong light, and soon adjust to rhythms of sleeping and waking. Gradually light in all its modulations is taken in, and with it the distinguishing of form and movement. Color adds its own variety of differentiation, distances can be gauged, and recognition is established. Changes of expression can be experienced and "understood." Tears communicate.

What the infant takes in with the eyes stimulates the whole physical apparatus, which may in time react with a kinetic spasm of pleasure, a veritable orgasm of delight. The arms and legs thrash around, the eyes glow, and sputtering, laughing sounds voice enthusiastic participation. When crying takes over, the eyes close and the body becomes rather quietly tense. The whole sensory system, thus, is indeed "fearfully and wonderfully made" and readying itself for the long journey of the life cycle.

Beginning with the second year, even when early nurturing has been maintained with optimal conditions for sensory growth, cultural restraints begin to move in more urgently.

I watched two youngsters on the beach recently, one a toddler just up on his feet and not too steady, the other a bit older with a wider range of skills and, therefore, a wider space in which to be adventurous. The toddler was wholly preoccupied with discovering sand. He caressed it, let it run through his fingers, tried it out with his toes, wiggled in it, and poured it on his tummy, completely absorbed. Then along came his mother with a toy truck and urged him to fill it with sand, suggesting as well that he use a small shovel to build a castle. He complied half-heartedly and then crawled away, again exploring and testing. His mother tried again, so eager to have a purposeful son achieving, constructing, or at least to have these appropriate toys she had supplied brought into the act.

When I moved away, it so happened that I saw an older child, a girl, who was standing in the waves—first the small ones, then, a bit farther out, jumping, splashing, her whole lithe body responsive and involved. And there was another mother speaking, out of an idle but unsubstantiated anxiety: "That's far enough now, dear—don't go out too far. The water is dangerous. Do be careful." That dangerous water was less than six inches deep; knee-high water was yards away.

These two small episodes, as well as numerous other more flagrant ones, remind us that we live in a nontactile, predominantly kinesthetically dull, success-ridden society. Here were these lovely, vital little creatures entirely occupied with just being, enjoying the present moment with all their lively senses in a delight-giving space. And weren't we all, once, just as eager to sense the world—and aren't we still more than a little envious? We should be more informed about these vital senses, know more exactly what makes up our sense endowment since, indeed, we all have been involved with these sensory antennae since our first heartbeats. To do this we will have to begin with a few more academic facts.

The organs of sense, we are told, develop epigenetically (that is, in a given order) in utero. At birth, then,
each infant comes into the world with a certain endowment of sense organs, and these vary genetically from
those of others. We are not all equally well endowed:
The organs of taste, smell, and tactile sensitivity vary
somewhat in their acuteness, and even blindness and
deafness occur. Gifted children, we have always con-
tended, are those whose senses are particularly acute; those
whose senses are somewhat less keen to begin with can,
with appropriate stimulation and under the care of trained
experts, increase the acuity of the organs with which they
have been endowed. When one sense organ is nonfunc-
tioning, the acuity of those remaining can be markedly
increased to an exceptional level through training and
concentration.

The final efficacies of the developed senses depend on
the reinforcement offered by the environment in the form
of appropriate stimuli and through the motivation provided by warm and encouraging human nurturing. The
word "appropriate" must be stressed, since overstimula-
tion, such as over-loud music, can damage the hearing
organs even as glaring lights can impair the eyes.

For the most part, all our senses respond to motion
inaugurated from outside the body: the ear to sound waves;
the eyes to the molecular movement of light; taste to
chemical changes in the mouth when a material element
is introduced; and smell to the movement of air into the
nostrils. Touch is movement introduced from the environment or initiated by the individual. Body movement,
which quite naturally involves all the other senses, results
from a synthesizing kinesthetic sense reaction. If the
stimulus comes from the exterior, as, for example, sooth-
ing or hurtful touch, the kinesthetic sense reacts by evok-

ing an appropriate muscle response, such as relaxing and moving closer or moving hastily away. This is also true for sensations arising in the interior of the body, such as hunger, thirst, or even satiation, where the reactions are largely involuntary.

Now, all our senses are certainly responding to stimuli, whether dully or acutely, at every living moment. Probably no individual has ever sharpened all these senses to their full potential, and our particular Western culture stresses sight and hearing, while touch, taste, smell, and kinesthesia are grossly undereducated.

When the phrase "to sense" is used, it means that all the senses are being tapped for information and that this results in what we call "perception." It is important to realize that all knowledge begins with sensory experience. The role of the senses, then, is to inform the mind. Perception will thus be as keen or as dull as the quality and the validity of the information the senses affirm. One might say it is only possible to be a really sensible person, to have good sense, if one is accurately informed by reporting senses that are keen and vital.

In other words, the sense information we have accrued through experience is the most personal and valid content of our minds. What we store up in our heads is the accumulation of experience made available to us through our senses. All the other information we select and gather might legitimately be classed as indirect knowledge based on what someone else has said or written. I suppose that the validity of the information thus gathered will be judged according to the authority of the voice heard—perhaps one that still nags from the past—or the believability and reputation of the author read. In due time, however, one learns that there is a choice and that the voice and the written word can be accepted or ignored; but it does take time to learn this, and children are particularly prone to being misled by the authoritarian voices of teachers and parents and by the printed word.

This is very important information for those who include creative activities in their lives—those most keenly sense-oriented experiences which offer the greatest challenge to the authenticity of our sensibilities. We can bring to this experience nothing really creative that is not totally our own, and this is essential to its uniqueness, its integrity. The creative experience demands of us only that which is genuinely our own—and all that we do have that is genuinely our own is our personal, accrued store of sense data. That is what we really know. The rest is all secondhand and debatable.

In order to adapt ourselves to everyday life, the senses must be developed for mere survival. Through the ages, human beings have stressed an ultimate form of expression unique to each sense; music and poetry became the arts of the ear; the visual arts the aesthetic media of the eye; sculpture and ceramics the arts of touch; dance the experience of motion motivated by the pure enjoyment of body movement. The education (sometimes re-education) of the senses, if this is undertaken for the pleasure in sharpened perception, can increase the satisfactions inherent in daily living, but can also open new and adventurous avenues of aesthetic experience. These experiences lead into the stimulating discovery of the world of materials and tools, offering apprenticeship in the surprising and always demanding processes of the arts.

One of the most rewarding by-products of pursuing any art activity is that the process itself results in more profound intelligence, a greater appreciation of materials, and respect for the lawfulness of all matter. For the first time, perhaps, one sees with a curious freshness the rings of the life-cycle pattern recorded in the grain of a slab of wood that must be observed with care in order to make the carving and shaping of it possible. With amazement, you may hear the unexpectedly clear tone of an empty, hanging flowerpot struck with a soft mallet. The sharpened eye and ear can thus recapture two of what we postulate to be the lost enchantments of childhood: the innocent eye and the innocent ear. As Herbert Read has said in his essay "The Innocent Eye":

> The only real experiences in life [are] those lived with a virgin sensibility—so that we only hear a tone once, only see a color once, see, hear, touch, taste and smell everything but once, the first time. All life is an echo of our first sensations, and we build up our consciousness, our whole mental life, by variations and combinations of these elementary sensations.*

The innocent eye, then, is surely the eye that perceives out of the pure pleasure of exercising its natural function with "virgin sensibility." Later, looking as well as hearing are no longer enough in themselves; things are named and categorized and divested of the wonder of their first impact on our senses. Looking and hearing can become a means to an end—mere tools. We lose the paradise of wonder and surprise and are left with a deep and abiding nostalgia.

To help us, in Robert Browning's words to "recapture that first fine careless rapture" of the fresh perception and wonder of childhood is surely *the* challenge for the artist. Albert Camus says more directly: "A work of man is only the long journeying to find again through the lab-

---

*Herbert Read, "The Innocent Eyes" in *Annals of Innocence and Experience*. London: Faber & Faber, 1940.

yrinth of art the two or three great images upon which, once, the heart first opened.''

Our own Walt Whitman has shown us a specific way back through the looking glass into the not really lost world of our own childhoods. He recalls his identifications with the things, the elements of his environment, through his capacity to know by becoming. This experience of active participation, of empathy with the things of the world, is recorded in his poems so that we are drawn into his young sensory perceptions in an extraordinary way.

> There was a child went forth every day,
> And the first object he looked upon, that object he
>     became,
> And that object became part of him for the day or a
>     certain part of the day.
> Or for many years or stretching cycles of years.*

Many other authors and poets have recalled their early childhood and youth with great authority and beauty, as indeed have musicians, dancers, dramatists, and painters. They point to the source and dare us to follow.

The wisest of wise men said, ''become like children,'' an injunction that perplexed one great intellectual of his day and has continued to challenge many towering minds since then. Mencius the Chinese sage said, ''The wise man retains his childhood habit of mind.'' He knew, of course, that this is supremely difficult to do, for it requires of us an attention, a relationship with the world and the

---

*Walt Whitman, ''There Was a Child Went Forth,'' *Leaves of Grass*, as quoted in L. Untermeyer, *The Poetry and Prose of Walt Whitman*. New York: Simon & Schuster, 1949.

people around us which we can at best only maintain for moments: to see the wholeness of the universe in a blade of grass and hear it in a bird song, and along with the wonder of this accept with humility a deep "childlike notknowingness."

In her book *The Ecology of Imagination in Childhood,** Edith Cobb, to whom I am indebted for this phrase, writes, "The sense of wonder is spontaneous, a prerogative of childhood. Wonder," she goes on to say, "is itself a kind of expectancy of fulfillment." She believes that the child by "moving pieces of his world into structure and pattern" learns to feel "the mystery but also the lawfulness of the cosmos."

Cobb also says that, long before such structuring is possible, "the baby's discovery of his hands and his delight at their reappearance in his line of vision are marked with a sense of wonder."

Yet wonder need not remain a prerogative of childhood, for the ancient Greeks recognized the role of wonder as "the cause of knowledge, the basis of cognition" (Plato). The "sense of wonder is the mark of the philosopher. Philosophy indeed has no other origin," Socrates says in the *Theœtetus*. And in our less philosophically oriented century, Kenneth Clark, speaking of creativity in the arts and its evolution in the individual, also discusses the role of perception in human development and "the light suffused into the mind by wonder." He argues that only after active experience with literature or art can this sense of wonder be captured in *adult* imagination. "We may not experience these illuminations very often in our busy adult lives, but they were common in our

---

*Edith Cobb, *The Ecology of Imagination in Childhood.* New York: Columbia University Press, 1927.

childhood, and given half a chance we could achieve them still."*

And who can forget the moment of wonder and fascination that Einstein described, recalling the moment his father made him the gift of a compass:

> A wonder of such nature I experienced as a child of 4 or 5 years, when my father showed me a compass. That this needle behaved in such a determined way did not at all fit into the nature of events, which could find a place in the unconscious world of concepts (effect connected with direct "touch"). I can still remember—or at least believe I can remember—that this experience made a deep and lasting impression upon me. Something deeply hidden had to be behind things.†

It would be presumptuous to compare our own perceptive capacities to those of a genius like Einstein. However, it might be well to find out how he was nourished and supported through his school years.

We are informed that Einstein had been a poor and a resistant student in school, and when he applied for admission to the Polytechnic Institute in Zurich, he was turned down. Either he did not pass the written prerequisites or his grades were too low. It was then decided that he should spend a year in the provincial Swiss Pestalozzi Institute. What were the fundamental principles introduced by Pestalozzi in 1770 that still motivated the teaching in the schools that bore his name?

---

*Sir Kenneth McKenzie Clark, *Moments of Vision.* Oxford, England: Clarendon, 1954.

†Gerald Holton, ed., Albert Einstein, "Autobiographical Notes," trans. by Paul Arthur Schilpp, in Paul Arthur Schilpp, ed., *Albert Einstein: Philosopher-Scientist.* Evanston, Ill.: Library of Living Philosphers, 1949, p. 9.

## Our Vital Resources: The Senses

We know that Johann Heinrich Pestalozzi was a passionate advocate of enlisting the senses in all learning procedures, and he deplored the custom of his day that forced six-year-old children into classrooms to sit at desks for hours, learning to read and write. He wanted elementary schools abolished, believing that children could follow his principles better at home with the simple guidance of their mothers.

Pestalozzi's first principle was that children should be taught to observe *(anschauen)*. The import of this word, however, did not suggest merely "looking": for him it included observing intently with each sense. Each object should be handled, smelled, tasted, listened to, and looked at from a variety of angles. One should be given the name of a thing only after all its properties that the senses can record have been absorbed. Slowly these sense impressions should be increased to include the many objects in the child's environment. Then a vocabulary can be developed to impress the attributes of the object's nature on the child's consciousness.

Pestalozzi encouraged the drawing of shapes using chalk on large slates, introduced measuring, and stimulated the awareness of a sense of proportion. Children, he felt, should not be required to make small lines with pens on small paper. He introduced various manual skills and sought teachers able to draw and sing, to weave and play instruments.

Sounds, he taught, should be fully "heard" before reading is learned so that language can more adequately express both rhythm and meaning. Writing should naturally follow proficiency in drawing. The conception of *form*, he said, would then simply follow the ability to bind together the sense information which had been gathered into a whole, an idea or conception—in other words, a *gestalt*.

Despite the derision of his contemporaries, he persisted in claiming that *anschauen,* to grasp with the senses, was the absolute foundation of all knowledge.*

We will do well to remember Einstein's account of his reluctance to talk: "My parents were worried because I started to talk so comparatively late, and they consulted the doctor because of it."†

He then also mentions a "peculiarity" of his, namely, that until the age of seven he used to repeat softly his own words and those of others—to *sound* them, as it were, to taste their sound.

His younger sister reports, too, how he spent hours in quiet play with building blocks and jigsaw puzzles, games of patient and solitary persistence, by which he seems to have trained his capacity to fit forms into one another, and we begin to see how the Pestalozzi approach to learning suited his temperament. Geometry, algebra, and, of course, arithmetic were approached with objects, forms, and proportions and not with tiny ciphers on paper.

By Einstein's time this method was highly developed for more advanced learning, and we can easily understand how this verification of his own learning process could lead Einstein's scientific curiosity to the astonishing consideration of, for example, the appearance of light waves to an observer who is keeping pace with their velocity.

He did go on to the Polytechnic Institute but even later, as Erik H. Erikson notes,

the resistance against enforced instruction, far from ever being "broken," became a deep and basic character

*Johann, Heinrich Pestalozzi, *How Gertrude Teaches Her Children.* London: George Allen & Unwin, Ltd., 1894.
†Holton, Einstein, "Autobiographical Notes," pp. 151–52.

trait that permitted the child and the youth to remain free in learning, no matter how slowly or by what sensory or cognitive steps he accomplished it. I see a connection here with what he later emphasized as *Begreiflichkeit* (comprehensibility), that is, an active and intuitive "beholding" as a necessary step in thinking. Could it be that the need to wait for such moments— that is, a delayed "I see!" phenomenon—had not permitted him to accept too early and too glibly the ways language has of prescribing meanings not really "grasped." And remember, one of his later most childlike and yet wisest sayings is that the most incomprehensible aspect of the world is its comprehensibility.*

One may wonder how many other people with less persistence and less understanding parents have floundered without fulfilling the promise of latent intellectual capacities because of the pressures of standardized curricula and methods. Could it not be that we underrate and underdevelop our senses throughout the school years and our lifetimes, as Pestalozzi maintained? He had a wonderful sense of humor. He now, no doubt, would find our veneration of Einstein not only rewarding but more than a little ironic.

Since Pestalozzi's time, great teachers like John Dewey and Maria Montessori have been aware of his precepts and have incorporated them in their own fashion. The best nursery school teaching manifests this new appreciation of his methods. However, I would like to express my homage to a present-day teacher who seemed to know instinctively what Pestalozzi taught. Rita de Lisi directed

*E. H. Erikson, *Psychoanalytic Reflections of Einstein's Centenary*, Part I, *The Victorious Child.* Princeton, N.J.: Princeton University Press, 1982.

an art experience for a group of preschool children in a "store-front school" for several years in Cambridge, Massachusetts, during the 1960s. Her approach was to present the children (and assistant teachers) with a carefully prepared sensory experience before encouraging any doing or making activity. Within walking distance of the store, for example, she would locate a garden that could be visited. The children and she observed the garden space and arrangement together and closely investigated the growing things on hands and knees. Then they moved up onto the back porch of the adjoining house and had a long-range view of the whole scene.

On return to the studio store, large sheets of paper were laid out on the floor, and each child had a separate space to work in, with a variety of colors. The paintings were so varied it was amazing to realize that all twelve children had seen the same garden. Their colorful and imaginative work was exceptionally vivid and alive.

On another occasion, a large variety of scrap materials of various textures was provided for investigation and observation by the children, who then made collages, using generous applications of glue. On another occasion, quantities of fishnets of various sizes were sensitively tested and observed. With all hands pulling together in a circle, the diamond-shaped spaces between the knots in a large net could be stretched thin or spread out. Hairnets were small enough to investigate singly or with the cooperation of a partner. Later, each child drew, with charcoal or paint, a net on a large sheet of paper, forming what he or she had observed. Filled with imaginative "fishes," these paintings were playful and brilliant with color.

The response of the children to all of these offerings was one of pleasurable anticipation and excitement, and the originality and diversity of the objects created were impressive.

*Our Vital Resources: The Senses*

Children are so often encouraged to produce paintings or clay objects in a creative class situation before their senses have been appropriately informed and stimulated by preliminary sensory experiencing so that unique perceptions can find meaningful form.

We have been discussing the work and the ideas of some of our most innovative thinkers. To what capacity do we ascribe the freshness of their contribution, of their insights? The mysterious phenomena of imagination may offer us the answer to this question. Susanne Langer nominates imagination for the "oldest mental trait that is typically human—older than discursive reason; it is probably the common source of dreams, reason, religion, and all true general observation. It is this primitive human power—imagination—that engenders the arts and is in turn directly affected by their products."* She assumes that one knows just what imagination is and how it relates to human sensory capacities. A dictionary provides us with one psychological definition of imagination: "The power to reproduce images stored in the memory under the suggestion of associated images or of combining former experiences to create new images." I would challenge this definition as being too limited since it focuses so narrowly on the visual, on images. In *this culture*, and at this historical moment, we are predominantly visually oriented, but the other five senses are there to play important roles and can be encouraged to participate much more than they do. Sounds do not necessarily evoke images of small black spots on lines or of particular instruments. When a breeze blows on the skin one feels a sensation but sees nothing tangible with eyes closed or open. Therefore, let us say, a definition of imagination might be: The power to *project* experience by means of the recall

---

*Susanne Langer, *Problems of Art*. New York: Scribners, 1957.

(remembering) of sensory components (members) stored in memory and evoked in the present by associated sensory stimuli or, one might say, by the combining of former perceptions to create the possibility of a new experience. The resulting *conception* is then formed by the relating of ideas or feelings to one another in a *pattern* which implies to conceive, to give birth to something new. "Thoughts and ideas, the fair and immortal children of the mind."* Edith Hamilton quotes this phrase from an ancient Greek source and it aptly expresses this parenting which we applaud as imagination.

The time for the nurturing of the senses and their expression in imaginative activity is early childhood—when young lives are not yet caught up in our striving, competitive culture. Should we not then deplore the growing tendency to begin to teach reading and writing and arithmetic in kindergarten? If imagination is the "oldest mental trait that is typically human," we must avoid becoming less-than-human technocrats.

Susanne Langer continues: "Self-knowledge, insight into all phases of life and mind, springs from artistic imagination. That is the cognitive value of the arts. It is, I think, at the very heart of personal education."

It is important to discover how our jaded senses can be revitalized so that as persons we may become more grounded, more centered in what we truly know, in that innermost core of our being. There is every reason to believe that this is possible. Those who have been deprived of one sense record that all others become more acute to take over greater responsibilities. Jacques Lusseyran, blinded in his eighth year, writes:

*Edith Hamilton, *The Greek Way*. New York: New American Library, 1930.

3 6

A blind person hears better, and that is as it should be, because he hears what he does not see. A blind person has a better sense of feeling, of taste, of touch. He should be told how much his senses keep in reserve for him. But first of all, it seems to me, it is necessary to point out to him the condition that leads to such a widening of the senses.

The condition isn't simply not seeing anymore. Neither does it mean that a new structure is given to the remaining senses. The necessary condition is much simpler; one has to be attending.

From just this "total attention" the seeing are constantly diverted. So are the blind, but not to the same degree. For them remaining attentive is a practical necessity, and this simple fact constitutes the first of their gifts.*

Attention: The senses demand their price! We must pay this overall attention or be unaware and uninformed. Every genuine artist knows this. All of us deserve to experience it in our daily lives on an ongoing basis, which brings us again to William James and his version of vital reserves. He was, of course, a dyed-in-the-wool Victorian, and although he does go so far in his essay as to mention "the emotions and excitements," the word "senses" is never used in his paper. However, what he does say is:

We are all to some degree oppressed, unfree. We don't come to our own. It is there, but we don't get at it. The threshold must be made to shift. . . . The normal opener of deeper levels of energy is the will. The difficulty is

*J. Lusseyran, *And There Was Light*. Boston: Little, Brown, 1963.

to use it, and make the effort which the word volition implies.*

James then describes a variety of ascetic exercises and other methods for harnessing the will and shifting gears. It is not a developmentally oriented thesis. However, attention demands vitality and concentration, which vary enormously in human beings. The range of observable vital responses from more maladjusted manifestation to what could be a measure of normal alert liveliness is a matter which concerns us all.

In infancy a vast difference may be observed between a lethargic baby and one with a high energy level. Premature infants are apt to appear apathetic and in need of quantities of sleep; those born to mothers who have ingested large amounts of narcotics, alcohol, or nicotine are apt to be slow in expressing normal needs. Some babies appear to be overactive and tense due to genetic factors or traumatic prenatal experience. In the initial adjustment of the infant, the birth experience itself may play a much greater role than has been previously understood. A wide normal range of vital energy and responsiveness exists between these extremes.

The keenness of the senses in those infants that are low in vitality may be potentially normal but understimulated, whereas the hyperactive baby and young child may have a very low threshold for sensory stimulus but normally keen senses. These factors tend to create a wide margin of difference in the responses of individuals to sensory stimuli in the first years of childhood and possibly throughout the life span. However, it is certain that the general physical vitality of the whole organism supports the activity of all the senses.

*William James, *On Vital Reserves.*

The uses, strains, and abuses of the senses throughout the adult years of the life span are too various and too numerous to consider here. But a number of general hazards which concern us all are socially maladaptive and may be underscored.

Glaring lights, small print, and television may negatively affect the eyes, beginning in childhood. The general use of eyeglasses has increased. Are they more in demand only because we are now technically better equipped to produce them?

We urgently need to discover how to care for vision from infancy on if we are to continue to exist in a technology which is so eye dependent. Strides could be made in improving the lives of all of us if more research could be undertaken on the prevention of sight loss.

The problem of the impairment of *hearing* may be an even greater one for everyone. It would be impossible to state with authority that hearing loss is now greater than previously, since today our technical methods of detection have improved so radically. Our urban world has become increasingly noisy. Heavy equipment and machine tools assault our ears, and planes disturb even rural areas. Since it is possible to be deafened by the sound of a bell at close range, it is more than probable that the capacity to hear is dulled by the high volume amplification of musical sound young people prefer.

Perhaps the only hope for prevention of hearing impairment is a clearer understanding of what the increased volume of noise and the amplification of sound are contributing to hearing impairment in all age groups of our modern world.

Keenness of the *sense* of *taste* and the saliva flow that makes this acuity possible do not change appreciably during the adult years under normal conditions. However, a decrease in saliva flow may occur with the deterioration of the tissue in the mouth due to a variety of causes. Drugs, smoke, and overuse of salt and sugar (and alcohol) are destructive to these tissues, and incur dental decay.

What this information offers concerning eating habits at the present time is arresting. Aside from drugs, alcohol, and cigarettes, all of which are used in great quantities in our many Western societies, there is sugar in almost everything that is packaged, canned, or bottled.

Because of a decreased keenness of taste, the capacity to *smell* is dulled. An increased aversion to all bodily odors and a high threshold for strong artificial perfumes is apparent to anyone monitoring the fashion advertising scene.

The sense of touch, so acutely responsive in infancy, is, in our society, both permissibly encouraged yet in other ways discouraged. Clothing is in general less restrictive than in the past, which allows the skin to "breathe," and on beaches exposure to sun and water is expected. But in other professional areas of activity both men and women conform rigorously to standard costumes. The casual arm around shoulder and waist, or hand holding, so observable in southern Europe and elsewhere, is for the most part frowned upon or questioned.

A produce display in a large shopping center is an odorless, plastic touch-safe area, each item only two-dimensional and unresponsive to finger selection. One woman was overheard advising another: "Go where the fruit flies are. Then you'll know it hasn't been sprayed and is ripe." Cookies and crackers are bought according to pictures on tightly wrapped packages. Other produce is coated with a shiny surface of wax and of one knows not what preservative. Altogether only a sterile, if ever so antiseptic, nonsensory experience is offered.

Pavement in all urban areas has demanded that feet,

once so sensitively related to the ground, now remain shod in close-fitting, hard-soled shoes.

Progress in one direction seems necessarily to bring with it deprivation in another, and these losses can be basic, like feet, and should cause concern.

*Memories* are the store of accrued sensory impressions, the perceptions that have shaped our minds and sharpened intelligence. To retain the capacity to remember, as we age, becomes then an important ingredient of mental alertness.

Sensory information is held briefly in storage upon receipt and is consistently retrieved by the process of paying it attention lest it be overlaid by newer incoming sense information. A constant sorting of input serves to give precedent to some categories of information, crystallizing them in relatively permanent long-term storage and relegating others to short-term memory.

This sorting of incoming sensory stimuli demands concentration and a capacity for quick and fluid evaluation. With time, the nervous system and muscular functioning decline in resilience. The ability to react with the speed necessary for dealing with great numbers of incoming stimuli is overtaxed. Fluid intelligence tends to decline, and with it short-term memory. However, crystallized intelligence, which results from long-term evaluation and selection supported by education and experience, continues to increase throughout the years of maintained vitality.

When fluid intelligence fails, compensation can be effected by a persistent focusing of attention, and motivation, which is required for such persistence, can be increased if environments and activities offer sufficient appropriate stimuli. Training does improve the capacity for short-term memory, and it may be possible to find even more sensitive and enjoyable ways (such as the arts and other creative activities) to stimulate concentration and thus prevent inappropriate memory loss.

The power to recall is one of the sensory vitalizers of any age, but especially of the later years of the life cycle. Although immediate facility in remembering names of people and places may become less sharp, it is amazing how precisely memories of things long passed may be brought to mind when yesterday's details of events seem blurred.

Oliver Sacks describes a middle-aged man who had lost his power of recollection for everything in his life beyond his nineteenth year. Not being able to remember yesterday, this morning, or even a few minutes ago, he was sadly isolated by his loss of integral experience of time and continuity. However, he did describe with animation "a full and interesting early life, remembered vividly, in detail and with affection."* Dr. Sacks speaks of his innocent wonder, his authentic amazement on being presented with a new idea or fact, such as a picture of the earth taken from the moon.

This lost man was able to find continuity and reality in an absorption in ritual—the ritual of the Mass—but also could reach a similar depth of attention in musical experience, in art, and could follow dramas with involvement. He found a preferred area of creative activity in the garden, where he never got lost or disoriented as he was apt to do elsewhere.

Kenneth Koch recorded the vividness of description in the poems of the old people with whom he had regular workshop sessions.† The power of expression of his stu-

---

*Oliver Sacks, *The Man Who Mistook His Wife for a Hat.* New York: Summit Books, 1985.

†Kenneth Koch, *I Haven't Told Anyone.* New York: Random House, 1977.

dents developed tremendously, as did their motivation to express their memories and feelings and to thus communicate with the other participants in the group. Robert Penn Warren, one of our most vital older poets, writes of the mystery of becoming:

> You had not, for instance, previsioned the terrible thing
> called love,
> Which began with a strange, sweet taste and bulbed
> softness while
> Two orbs of tender light heaved there above.
> Sometimes your faces got twisted. They called it a smile.

And the final verse of the poem continues:

> Yes, you must try to rethink what is real. Perhaps
> It is only a matter of language that traps you. You
> may find a new way in which experience overlaps
> words. Or find some words that make the truth come
> true.*

A word craftsman of consummate skill can evoke recall with a few phrases. There are, however, evocative roads to recall other than that "of language that traps you." Recently such means was brought to my attention: An old woman sat alone and withdrawn in a group at a hospital where Christmas was being discussed. She volunteered nothing and on questioning only answered, "I not remember." After much persuasion and teasing with exact questions concerning what, at home in Poland, they had cooked for the holiday, she reluctantly named a dish. Then

---

*Robert Penn Warren, from *New and Selected Poetry*. © 1985 by Robert Penn Warren. Reprinted by permission of Random House, Inc.

"How did you cook it? What did you do?" brought on an at first reluctant demonstration concerning a big pot and long spoon and slow, steady stirring of something very thick "that got thicker and thicker." As she bent and swung her arms around and around, her face became flushed, and she began to talk about the food, the family, the friends, and eventually about a sleigh ride and her father's horses. Kinesthetic memory is a splendid backtrack, it seems, to childhood.

And why should one assume that the old are completely occupied with reflection? With the world around them consistently stimulating their very present senses, recalling old sense experiences, and offering further projections of the imagination, their minds can be creative and permanently active. For remembering to be creative the recollecting must be drawn up toward us into the present. One can drown in the Lake of Mnemosyne, those deep waters of memory where one should only drink to be refreshed. Speaking of his observations in an English village, Ronald Blythe reported: "often the intensity of non-stop remembrance is not refreshing. It exhausts, and one old lady longed for a visitor to 'stop my thoughts of my life going around and around, and wearing my out.' "*

Nostalgia is debilitating. The problem, when it exists, lies in the environment, in the lack of sensory stimuli for the older individual—not necessarily in his or her "normatively" restricted capacities.

It is no wonder, then, that all authorities on the problems as well as the normative aspects of aging agree that general physical participation in activities of all kinds is the single most important requirement for the prevention of premature aging. Since all the senses must be involved

---

* Ronald Blythe, *The View in Winter*. Middlesex, England: Penguin Books Ltd., 1979.

in kinetic activity, they in turn are stimulated by the active participation of all parts of the body. Greater keenness of perception may thus motivate the awareness and attentive observing which support vital involvement.

The question is: How does one best orient oneself throughout the life-cycle span in order to support, maintain, and even enhance the possibility of keeping the senses alive and acute? What activities promote the necessary involvement and are universally time-honored ways of enriching life? The answer is, of course, that creative activities in general, and specifically all art-oriented making and doing throughout life, offer this fulfillment.

# The Vitalizing
# Properties
# of Creative Activity

A bronze figure of the god Shiva, arms outspread, poised in ecstatic dance; a Greek urn elegantly formed and patterned with figures and leaves; or a copy of Michelangelo's *David* presiding over a busy square in Florence: How shall we describe the feeling that wells up in us as we "behold" them? In India, they speak of *darshan*. This experience is sought as one might seek a blessing, and found in the presence of great persons whose spirit pervades the whole surrounding area. Great works of art, be they artifact, performance, or poem, share this aura, speaking as they do with authority and saying yes to our striving to transcend human limitations by means of superhuman creative effort.

Creativity involves generating that which is new, original, unique. We live all too often in molds, tight grooves, and to find the freedom necessary to break out of these restrictions we need a sense of playfulness which allows experimentation and change. The first nudging of the mold may only result in a slight widening of a crack, a minute addition to or subtraction from a habitual pattern. A mere ripple of change may result which, with continued pressure, could become a real breakthrough. Change, admittedly, is hazardous. It serves both construction and destruction. But the uncracked mold stultifies growth and breeds stagnation.

Let us consider this quality of playfulness that defies categorization by cautiously, even playfully, approaching it from a number of directions.

## Play and Playfulness

The word *play* has an amazing range of meanings. Just a glance at the dictionary gives us "to play a role," "to play a game." These are experiences we all know well, but "to play the piano" is of a different order and achieved only with discipline. "To play fast and loose," "to play into someone's hands," and "to play up or down" are metaphors that demand definition. Medieval English gives us *pleien*—to leap for joy, dance, rejoice, be glad. For me this active expression of a leap for joy, however minuscule, represents most persuasively the sense of playfulness.

Performing even a very moderate leap calls for several prerequisites: buoyance, a firm footing for taking off, a relaxed but steady landing, and a certain bouncing lightness throughout. One must move freely within prescribed limits and with no serious purpose. A flock of circling birds, windsupported, riding each gust or resisting with the mere tip of a wing, suggests the carefree receptive quality necessary.

How do we come by this experience? How do we sustain it? How do we keep ourselves from blocking it?

Watch little children play—two- or three-year-olds. If you are lucky, you will observe them on a beach, because sometimes parents are relaxed enough there to let them explore on their own. Their hands touch lightly a shell or a piece of driftwood and they finger each material with care, investigating, probing, experiencing—with no agenda. They toy with a piece of colored plastic as if it were the rarest of lovely shells, since they are as yet unprejudiced about the comparative value of things. It's a wide-open world full of delights, with waves, breezes, and beach grasses, as carefree and spontaneous as the small adventurers themselves.

And what does one need for such a carefree probing of the moment and place where one happens to be? As we suggested earlier, acute senses are needed as guides and the undivided attention which is natural to a child engrossed in discovery, plus an unawareness of time. Carefree playing doesn't emerge in the tension of hurry. Hurry and play are incompatible.

But there are other incompatibles, and if we think about some of them perhaps we may come closer to play. Let me suggest prejudgment—prejudice—as the first stumbling block, because it calls for immediate classification or categorizing and thus a limitation of scope. It implies a no. It's a stop sign. Consider the child and the piece of plastic on the beach. Imagine our small investigator taking a handful of shells, including the plastic, to her parent for sharing and receiving a reaction such as "Ugh, that old piece of plastic is nasty, but shells are fun to arrange." Well, to the curious youngster that difference is of little importance and it will be a long time, although soon enough, before her experiences begin to take on the evaluating quality that is so dulling to play.

As Herbert Read pointed out, if naming and sorting come too early they detour the curious, open sensing that is the basis of real knowing—of keen observation.* A child must learn to distinguish, but in the process parents often dull the pleasure of discovery, the fun of sorting out and arranging without bias. As adults, we do this to ourselves consistently, partly to save time and also because it has just become a habit. And in the same way we do shut off ideas, refuse to hear what we have classified out, and thus are in danger of becoming unresilient and inflexible.

Certainly drivenness is also unlikely to provide any relaxed waste of time, the kind of moment when a sudden idea like "why not" or "perhaps" or "what if" may just pop up. There is tension in drivenness—probably a tight schedule with some often overrated product or goal in view, generating anxiety. These pressures all preclude playful thought or casual experimental action.

But the most fundamental prerequisite of playfulness is that it must be self-activated. Coercion freezes the impulse to improvise spontaneously. A leap might conceivably be performed on command, but it would at best be only a disciplined gymnastic feat; note the intense, sometimes even grim, faces of Olympic athletes and the set expressions of ballet dancers.

What, then, are the essential elements of playfulness? Since we live in a culture in which the predominant measure of success is power and the accumulation of wealth with as little waste of energy as possible, why am I trying to promote—even celebrate—playfulness? How can playfulness be of value?

Science without inventiveness is only a technique. It is

---

*Herbert Read, "The Innocent Eye," in *Annals of Innocence and Experience*. London: Faber & Faber, 1940.

closely linked to art in that basic discoveries have been dependent on a spirit of play. Building with blocks, observing a compass with fascination, and ruminating about trains and flies (how can one calculate a fly's speed when it is speeding along in a train?) culminated in Einstein's theory of relativity. By the world's standards, he was anything but a success to begin with, but he managed not to let himself be hurried and to protect his own creative integrity with courage and persistence.

The hardheaded logical thinking which our schools promote is an increasing necessity in a technological society. It leads to a consistent need for computers, a dependence which is the outgrowth and demand of technology. But a bridge connecting these values and the enduring human values which transcend even a materialistic culture is essential, however difficult this may be. Children teach us and bring us back to these values with their open curiosity and unprejudiced awareness.

The prerequisites for playful thinking, feeling, and acting can be singled out. Time must not only be less pressing, but some time must be available, separate from the ordinary demands of daily life, to be valued for its own sake. Oddly enough, what this takes is discipline and awareness so that a slower pace can be maintained at least part of the time. It may even mean having to get up earlier to provide a little more leeway, a longer day. But no matter how much time there is, it is essential to come to that state of awareness in which the senses are alive and keen, imagination is free to play, and there is that openness for credulity which makes connections possible.

Fantasy, spinning tales, is surely a natural attribute of playfulness. This legacy from childhood needs nurturance throughout the life stages. Without imagination, we remain too firmly bound to time and place. Many of us assume that high adventure and great deeds are played out in the mysterious land of somewhere else. But we need not go so far away—only far enough to resist habit, venturing a little beyond ourselves so that the unconscious, that powerful source of imagination, may emerge. One of the great virtues of playfulness and of humor is an awareness of opposites, of contradictions. If you can see that the circus clown who courts disaster in his big shoes and oversized clothes, with his painted-on smile and trusting eyes, is completely in charge of his world as well as of us, that is thinking and feeling simultaneously in opposites. Paradox may result in laughing and crying at the same time, for it reaches the heart, the deepest source of feeling.

But the openness to look beyond the obvious and to consider what you see receptively is at the root of playful thinking, feeling, and action. It is part of taking a chance, getting out of line—daring, perhaps, to make a "fool" of yourself.

We must also think creatively about the space in which we live, if we are to be free of stereotypical patterns. *A Room of One's Own* is the powerful title that Virginia Woolf used for her book about creativity. A room to oneself is a great luxury, especially if that space is really one's own. However, I have often marveled at the difference in atmosphere in the homes of practicing artists and other more sedate dwellings. The word *sedate* is appropriate since it derives from the Latin *sedare*, to sit. Practically any room in an artist's home can be used for creative work; in fact, they evoke such activity. All children and many of the rest of us need more than sitting space to allow for doing and making of whatever variety.

I am not advocating disorder, although that itself can include a surprising awareness on the owner's part of just where everything is. Jean Piaget, we are told, would never let anyone clean or tidy his study, which was piled high with papers, although he knew precisely where everything was. But a painful orderliness, cleanliness, and setness in space can be stultifying. "The well-kept house gives evidence of a misspent life" (unknown, perceptive author). Space, light, materials, and tools are requisites for creative activities, and this space must be flexible and simple, stimulating and inviting.

This is not the pattern of life in suburbia, and city housing has become increasingly crowded. But many artists manage to create such space, and lucky are the children in their households.

I have a fantasy about the interior of the Mozart family's house in Salzburg. That it was always alive with music, we can take for granted, and also that in utero those children were already living with muted harmonious sounds. There were spinets and harpsichords, but no piano forte in those days. When Wolfgang was two and his sister six, I can visualize that small interior full of instruments in great variety taking up most of the space and a real litter of papers with music scores spread everywhere. Poor Mrs. Mozart; Austrian housewives are fastidious, but music was the center of life as well as the necessary bread and butter in the Mozart household.

House plans in architectural journals suggest that kitchens are becoming increasingly popular. Is it now the liveliest place in the house, where things are being done, the place "where the action is"?

## Things

When we consider the play of children, we quite naturally focus on *doing* and *making*. Making involves things and materials; doing suggests the innumerable physical activities in which vital, growing bodies delight. What are some of the meanings that *things* may have for children?

In our modern, Western world toys are too often cheaply made, easily broken, and discarded. When they are of better workmanship they are apt to be either acquired in such abundance that they clutter and become a burden or merely something to boast about. Often, however, the very young will select an object and bestow on it a special significance, a faithful attachment. Rainer Maria Rilke has described this important "thing" relationship of childhood as follows:

> If possible, out of practice and grown-up as your feelings are, bring them back to any one of your childhood's possessions, with which you are familiar. Think whether there was ever anything nearer to you, more familiar, more indispensable than such a thing. Whether everything else—except it—was not capable of acting unkindly or unjustly toward you, of frightening you with pain, or confusing you with uncertainty? If, amongst your early experiences, you knew kindness, confidence and the sense of not being alone—do you not owe it to that thing? The first time you shared your little heart, as one shares a piece of bread which must suffice for two, was it not with a thing?*

These are the words of a grown man, who carried with him the detailed memory of early experiences of uncertainty, pain, and loneliness and the consolation offered and consistently maintained by a thing. Not surprisingly, as an adult with such clear and sensitive memories, he

---

*Rainer Maria Rilke, *Where Silence Reigns.* © 1978 by New Directions Publishing Corp. trans. by G. Graig Houston. All rights reserved.

wrote a series of "Ding Gedichte," literally "thing poems," in their homage.

Rilke had been working in the studio of Auguste Rodin in a secretarial capacity. Together they conceived the idea of empathetically extracting poems from things and materials in the same manner—Rodin approaching a piece of marble, studying it perceptively to see what might be hidden within, and Rilke walking the streets of Paris observing and ruminating about the objects he encountered. That must have been an awesome atelier where Rodin's hands deftly discovered, uncovered, and yielded fabulous forms of stone and Rilke gave voice to the praising of the "ordinary things" he had discovered and appreciated so sensitively.

In the essay in which he discusses his reaction to things, Rilke speaks of "the smiling and the weeping which lie hidden in much-worn jewels," and the "intimate, the touching, the deserted, thoughtful aspect of many things which . . . moved me deeply by their beautiful participation in human living."*

Isn't this one of the revered aspects of old things, of heirlooms in particular, that they offer continuity to our lives? Things that we see and touch recall for us the loves and concerns, real or imagined, of those who touched and knew them well, valued and preserved them. Most things are disposed of either casually or carefully during a lifetime. Some enchantment preserves special things, perhaps beauty or craftsmanship, even a personal sentiment that the owner longed, in some way, to pass on as a thread from the past. Remembering serves integration; it makes one whole and is an aspect of wisdom.

In another essay, Rilke makes an amazing statement about dolls:

*Rilke, "Some Reflections on Dolls," in *Where Silence Reigns.*

*I don't get this. re read later, but I do remember w/ lac my baby doll.*

I know it was necessary for us to have things of this kind which acquiesced in everything. The simplest love relationships were quite beyond our comprehension, we could not possibly have lived and had dealings with a person who *was* something; at most, we could only have entered into such a person and have lost ourselves there. With the doll we were forced to assert ourselves, for, had we surrendered ourselves to it, there would then have been no one there at all. It made no response whatever, so that we were put in the position of having to take over the part it should have played, or having to split our gradually enlarging personality into part and counterpart; in a sense, through it to keep the world, which was entering into us on all sides, at a distance. The things which were happening to us incomprehensibly we mixed in the doll as in a test tube, and saw them there change colour and boil up. That is to say, we *invented* that also, it was so abysmally devoid of phantasy, that our imagination became inexhaustible in dealing with it.*

In our goal-oriented hurry we so overestimate what we call reality that we even speak of fantasy deprecatingly. This, if we push it to the extreme, as cinematology and television seem to be doing, can only be impoverishing. How reluctant will we become to be even temporarily without visual and auditory stimuli? Restaurants and shops, even hospital rooms and doctors' waiting rooms, testify to this constant demand for canned sound. Quiet places are becoming more and more difficult to find— where one can either concentrate or let the mind and fantasy be free and floating. Rilke then goes on to add a

---

*Rilke, "Some Reflections on Dolls."

salient and especially thought-provoking idea about the doll:

> It was silent, then, not deliberately, it was silent because that was its constant mode of evasion, because it was made of useless and entirely irresponsible material, was silent, and the idea did not occur to it to take some credit to itself on that score, although it could not but gain great importance thereby in a world in which Destiny, and even God Himself, have become famous above all because they answer us with silence. At a time when everyone was still intent on giving us a quick and reassuring answer, the doll was the first to inflict on us that tremendous silence (larger than life) which was later to come to us repeatedly out of space, whenever we approached the frontiers of our existence at any point.*

And he ends with the question, "Are we not strange creatures to let ourselves go and to be induced to place our earliest affections where they remain hope less?"

It is humbling to accept the evidence that the extremity of this man's loneliness could have found voice finally in such an outpouring of sensuous prose and poetry.

Like all attachments, a child's relationship to things comes out also in hatefulness and frustration. With things that cannot reciprocate, there is no mutuality, no response to our human need for receiving as well as for giving. Sometimes this frustration becomes intolerable. A two-year-old playing with his toys in his own room can angrily throw out the window the most cherished companions of other moments, of other days. Another youngster, whose

*Rilke, "Some Reflections on Dolls."

devotion to a certain teddy bear is conspicuous, can hang this bear by its neck off the railing of a small porch until it "behaves" and the child's frustration has worn off. Of course, such acting out may be the expression of disgust and fury at the omnipotent adults in the child's environment. However, parents cannot be so easily disposed of, and are also desperately needed. Toys may get broken, but they never retaliate.

We never entirely outgrow "such childish ways." The gift from someone with whom we are "out of love" quite loses its grace, and we look for ways to dispose of it or hide it. And is it not amazing how the presence of a lost object lingers on? How we search for it and how important it becomes in our memories? This attachment could be considered regrettable but is also understandable because things often represent extensions of our very selves.

For our purposes, the essential aspect of things is, in fact, their transcendence of personality. They exist in their own right, and imagination can endow them with a variety of meanings. But these meanings don't necessarily adhere, and things revert to being just what they are as soon as they are left alone. Imaginative play is, of course, the privileged magic of children, and the toys they cherish provide release from incongruities and frustrations which cannot be verbalized. The panda bear or crib blanket or doll is a consistent "other" which is endowed with deep affection when people fail, as even those with the best intentions invariably do. As Rilke phrases it, "This being-less-than-a-thing, in its utter irremediability, is the secret of its superiority."*

Rilke was writing prose and poetry early in the twentieth century. He was young, introspective, and strug-

*Rilke, "Some Reflections on Dolls."

gling to come to terms with problems evoked by his extraordinary childhood. When he wrote the quoted passages he was in his late twenties.

Zbigniew Herbert, a Polish poet, writing now at the end of the century, has also turned his attention to "poems on objects," but with another focus and motivation. Disillusioned about humankind and our capacity to cope with history and political power, he praises that quality in the object that is free of history and its false postures. "In Herbert's work a space filled with human struggles and suffering gives objects their background, and thus a chair or table is precious simply because it is free of human attributes and, for that reason, is deserving of envy," Czeslaw Milosz* tells us, who quotes the following poem by Herbert in one of his Charles Eliot Norton lectures (1981–1982):

## Pebble †

The pebble
is a perfect creature
equal to itself
mindful of its limits

filled exactly
with a pebbly meaning

with a secret which does not remind one of anything
does not frighten anything away does not arouse desire

---

* Czeslaw Milosz, *The Witness of Poetry*. Cambridge, Mass.: Harvard University Press, 1983.

† "Pebble" copyright © 1968 by Zbigniew Herbert. Translation copyright © Czeslaw Milosz and Peter Dale Scott, 1968. From *Selected Poems* by Zbigniew Herbert, published by The Ecco Press in 1986. Reprinted by permission.

its ardour and coldness
are just and full of dignity

I feel a heavy remorse
when I hold it in my hand

and its noble body is permeated by false warmth

Pebbles cannot be tamed
to the end they will look at us
with a calm and very clear eye

The pebble is "mindful of its limits," that awareness
which is the true humility accompanying the accurate
perception of our capacities. And Herbert ends with an
allusion to the verifying eye-to-eye contact which, from
infancy on, we consistently seek. This is a poem to be
studied like a koan, for its short statements add up to an
indictment of our vaunted human strengths.

I offer you a third poem about an object by Wallace
Stevens*:

## Anecdote of the Jar

I placed a jar in Tennessee
And round it was, upon a hill.
It made the slovenly wilderness
Surround that hill.

The wilderness rose up to it,
And sprawled around, no longer wild.
The jar was round upon the ground
And tall and of a port in air.

*Copyright 1923, renewed 1951 by Wallace Stevens. Reprinted from
the *Collected Poems of Wallace Stevens*, by permission of Alfred A.
Knopf, Inc.

It took dominion everywhere.
The jar was gray and bare.
It did not give of bird or bush,
Like no thing else in Tennessee.

This bare, gray, round thing, once placed "upon a hill" is activated, claims its place, a recent interloper. The word chosen for "the thing" is a noun-verb—may we assume that it is empty, but open, receptive, in that great spaciousness?

We are told its location, Tennessee, but would otherwise unfailingly have recognized that wild land, that "slovenly wilderness" that we know and of which we are.

The starkness of the lines recalls to our ears the crisp answers of country people to interrupting, talkative passersby: "If I was to go to Hartville Corners, I wouldn't start from here."

Should we be cautioned about where and what to place in wild, sprawling spaces? Is it well to be aware of the doing in just being, of the import, the impact, of placement?

I hear a challengingly blunt American tone in these short, crisp lines. The form is terse and ornery, and yet completely right—perfection. Conspicuously American, yet claiming both the old rhymed privilege and the new "free-form" rhythms of a still untamed Tennessee.

At any age we maintain our bonds with things. Nostalgically, we cling to them because they offer us continuity and a sense of relatedness to the ever-receding past. They strengthen an empty sense of identity and personal style, and are often confused with our sense of our own value. We cling to them, in fact, to offset our own insecurities: Money buys things that we wear, like symbols of power and prestige, to mark our importance, to promote a false sense of identity. The world, however, is rich with things that belong to everyone and readily stimulate our sense-oriented creativity. The genuine appreciation of the unique validity of things as our poets have recreated them for us endows all these objects with new meaning and enriches us with the memorable strength and grace of their poetry. We should remind ourselves here that the word *poet* is Greek in origin, meaning simply "to make" *(poiein)*. Thus all artists are poets and all poets are "makers"—makers of things, even poems. There is, to be sure, a gulf of essential difference in meaning which separates the original, unique handmade object from the manufactured, accurately repeatable one. Actually the thing that is patentable is the machine which produces the object. Hands themselves and minds do not qualify. There is an ancient saying from the Far East stating that the uniqueness and authenticity of handmade things is verifiable by even minute flaws, barely perceptible fingerprints in clay, for example, and the unevenness of texture in fabric.

## Materials and Tools

I would submit that materials are of a different order than things, since we all live inextricably in a matrix of matter. Things are made out of materials and, therefore, matter is more basic, and it is in this sense that I would like to present some of its intrinsic qualities.

The oldest toys to have been found the world over, gathered from archaeological digs, were fairly recently exhibited together in the Rockefeller Museum in Jerusalem. Most of them are scaled-down imitations of everyday objects and animals which have been unearthed in children's tombs: rattles, tops, pull toys, and sometimes the tattered remains of rag dolls.

A new toy is being constructed at this very moment by

a little girl sitting in the grass outside my window. She has bound two twigs together, added a shorter third, and separated the lower "legs" and upper "arms," leaving the third with a small cluster of leaves as head. At this moment she is spreading the soft leaves of a flowering yellow daisy bush into a kind of hula skirt for her new doll. It is charming, and in her hands it takes on a lively meaningfulness. This creative young person is quite small and obviously not yet in school. Her pleasure is also mine as I watch and wish she might always maintain her inventive relationship to the matter nature provides around her.

In this unpredictable and inconsistent world, a creative man or woman is enviable. He or she works with materials, and they offer their consistent, predictable lawfulness as a basis for their relationships, but a thorough experiential knowledge of the attributes of the material being handled is necessary. How does wood grow, for example? What variety is being used; how has it been cut, dried, and finished; and how do its particular rules differ from others? How does it respond to various techniques and tools? Secure in this background knowledge, the artist is free to proceed in complete confidence, provided the necessary skills have been mastered. He or she learns to love the chosen material, to study it with intimate attention and with as deep a wish to bring out its innate beauty as to make manifest the personal vision that will give it form.

Indeed, materials never fail. The artist is responsible for the selection of the material for a given project. If more is demanded of the material than it can perform, then it will prove to have been inappropriately selected. Informed selection is a mandatory requirement for the selector: There is no question where the responsibility lies. The verdict is always clear and just. Where else in life can one with such complete confidence face one's own limitations so squarely?

When materials teach us, they do so silently—without praise or blame. Quietly and with utmost integrity, they abide by the lawfulness of their own nature, responding to the touch and skill of the hands. Unlike the most even-tempered, well-disposed human teacher, they never get upset, angry, or even indignant. They do not have an agenda. They neither encourage nor discourage one's efforts. They promise one thing. They do not make promises and then change their minds. By virtue of their lawfulness, they give assurance of a predictable process and encourage commitment to further learning. Thus, dealing with the inherent beauty of materials and their unfailing reliability can involve us in a deeply healing process.

Some crafts rely entirely on the skill of hands. Our ancestors knew more of hand potential and skill than we do today, for we have developed tools. It is fascinating to observe the concerned care of artists for their tools. They polish, hone, and touch them with such respect and appreciation that the onlooker seems to be observing an intimate ritual. And so it is, for each prized tool will be lovingly handled, may perhaps be wrapped in deerskin or hung on the wall like a decorative object of special beauty.

We are told that in Japan, where houses are still hand fashioned throughout, the master carpenters spend two-thirds of their time caring for their tools and one-third using them. When questioned, they answer with asperity that only perfect tools produce perfection of workmanship. This cannot be denied, and skilled artists wisely devote much time to the care of these faithful co-workers.

In fact, all of the processes involved are extremely time

consuming. Creative activity has no respect for time as modern life values it. A greedy, premature productivity offers only a false sense of accomplishment. Slow exploration and experimentation over a long period of time with the material is the only way one gains command of a craft—plus, of course, that due payment of complete attention which we discussed earlier. Let me share an experience with you.

I witnessed an interesting demonstration at a regional craft conference. A very fine potter was speaking to a group of artists about her work. She had agreed to throw a pot for us, and we watched attentively as she centered the clay on the wheel and with expert skill began to mold and raise the form, a process that never loses its miraculous quality. She turned the wheel, steadied her hands, and the clay stretched smoothly up and up. There was a good deal of tension in the audience, but not a word was spoken, and only some breathy sounds of suspense were audible.

As she finished off the rim with cautious fingers, the whole top collapsed and everyone groaned. The potter sighed. Then, she turned to us slowly and said, "Well, I didn't give it my undivided attention. I was too aware of the time and of your expectations and just lost contact with the clay." She gently touched the slumping pot and said, "Sorry"—not to us, but to the clay.

This artist knew that what was essential was her full attention to the process and that she had been distracted by her audience. For a performer another set of rules applies. There it is appropriate for the performer to some degree to play for audience attention. In this case her relationship and her attention belonged on the clay and the developing pot; recognizing this, she acknowledged her failure.

## Process

It would be impossible to discuss the healing properties of creative activities in all our lives without undertaking to clarify the role that process plays and why it must be consistently stressed. The idea, the conception, is a gift of the imagination. The process is the disciplined work of manifesting that conception, uniquely and with integrity.

The modern world lays such emphasis on the work *product* and stresses productivity so relentlessly that process is only seen as a means to this end. The most highly approved process is one that is fast, efficient, and cheap.

But this question of process should be a matter of great concern to all those who are interested in fostering creative activities. Where no products are exhibitable in the form of saleable artwork or craftwork that can be merchandised at competitive prices, the support for art training becomes unavailable.

It has been said, and it is true to a point, that to produce crafts of questionable quality and be successful in selling them is valuable because it offers a great boost to the self-esteem of the apprentice craftsman. However, it also can lead very soon to a sense of personal deflation when it becomes obvious that only limited skills and values have been developed. In that sense, overpraise of the product in any art undertaking is patronizing and does a disservice to the person involved. A teacher of the arts can readily find words of appropriate support for a pupil who needs encouragement without falling into the trap of bolstering morale with false praise.

Then what is it, exactly, that should win praise and be encouraged in the work of one who is learning?

The role of the artist-instructor is to explain and demonstrate a process. This process is of course based on an intricate understanding of the medium, the materials, and the tools involved.

In the dictionary, we are told that a process is "a series of progressive and interdependent states by which an end is attained." The word *series* suggests ongoing sequential states or stages (as in epigenesis), and these are characterized by progress and interdependence. One proceeds in stages in every project of making and doing, whether it involves laying out a garden, making a bookshelf, or throwing a pot. First the idea must take shape, then the plan. After that, the materials and tools must be prepared. The work moves ahead in a series of steps, each dependent on the preceding one. There is a sense of progress, and although the steps are sequential they build upon one another. All the senses are involved and each stage offers great opportunity for learning. Is an idea feasible and within one's capacities? Can a viable plan be made? Are the materials and tools available?

But this is all just the planning stage. When the preparations are made, and the material is at hand, a new process begins. With whatever skill they have acquired, the hands now are touching, feeling, grasping; the eyes are keenly observing, guiding and focusing attentively on every move and shift of light. In fact, the whole body is aligned and concentrated on whatever action is demanded, naturally and spontaneously becoming entirely involved in the project. Other thoughts and concerns are set aside, and if time comes to mind it is only to observe how it is flying.

The dictionary, however, goes on to say that this procedure—this process in time—"brings about a series of changes as a natural outgrowth." How could one better express what happens both to the material and to the maker and doer? The material has become transformed into a new creation; the maker and doer has matured and grown in stature.

It is the role of the artist-instructor to oversee every step of the way. Experimentation, which is time taking, is nevertheless a vital ingredient of learning. It can be playful and yet seriously increase the understanding of the material and the development of skillful hands. Each failure is a further step in the learning process. The dedicated artist-teacher conveys the point of view that the process itself is the most valuable and pleasurable part of the project regardless of the outcome. The plan must be viable from the point of view of the capacities of the apprentice involved; if not, it must be modified or additional skills perfected.

The final product may be satisfying or disappointing, but the experience has made its mark, and what has been learned in skill, judgment, and patience can provide a firmer footing for the next project.

If the craftsperson or artist works consistently with one medium, these steps, of course, become routine, and materials and tools are prepared and at hand. He or she oversees the process with the attentive, eagle eye of the professional. But the role of the instructor is to make the process known and clearly understood. If the process is carried out with attentive care, and the product communicates some aspect of the maker in its own unique language, it surely is praiseworthy. This product may be as unassuming as a well-made bead, a braid of bright-colored wool, or a practical, well-proportioned book marker. If it is an original and unique expression of its maker, and if it exemplifies an appropriate use of the material and thus maintains a certain integrity, it is worthy of justified respect and appreciation.

Process is, I would like to stress, one of those words we cannot slight when we speak of art—or growth, for that matter. The healing properties of the experience are bound into the process. However, if because of its integrity, its vision, its skillful production it succeeds in communicating with others, the artist-craftsman will feel verified and exhilarated.

## Form

What could be the source of our sense of form except nature itself? Every natural thing is designed by eons of time with utmost economy to fulfill its role in the ecology of planet earth. Everything in nature *proceeds* to accomplish the development of its prescribed form. Man's prescribed form development is modified by his culture and technically re-formed environment because he does not belong exclusively to one natural or cultural setting—one matrix. His autobiography thus becomes his individual form. A human life may therefore be dedicated to consistent, sometimes passionate, effort to re-form natural materials, to give form to movement in space and time, or to formulate science theory, each according to its own sense of order.

Watch a small child playing alone. Observe how she attends to the natural forms in her surroundings, and then quite spontaneously becomes the poet—the maker—to give form to the materials within her reach. This is preceded by a testing, a sensual investigation of the matter at hand. Into this activity she pours the energy of her curiosity and her will to do and to make. Thus controlled by the *molding strictures of time and space* and the limitations of muscular sensory coordination, she forms her creation.

This sounds, I am sure, like a very high-toned way of describing the construction of a child's sand castle or the stick doll described earlier. However, if I used these words to convey how Picasso approached his studio and began his work, the words chosen might seem more appropriate. Yet I am convinced that Picasso proceeded with his sand castles exactly as he later proceeded with his great works of art. That the product is of a different order of sophistication is due not to the impulse to form the material, but to the accrued perceptual experience and coordinated skill of the mature artist.

What are these "molding strictures of time and space" within which our imaginative vitality and our physical energy function whenever we undertake to create—to make?

We live closely with body time, that earliest timing of which we become aware. Prenatally, the regular pulse of heartbeat, that of mother and infant, is sensed and becomes audible. Later, breathing assumes its rhythm, as do all the other bodily functions. We all share these time elements, as well as the more cosmic shifts from night to day and the great seasonal shifts of solstice and equinox. The sounds and rhythms that reach us from our environment expose us to an almost unlimited variety of stimuli; what these are and how we deal with them is personal and idiosyncratic. But in whatever ways we may develop our personal sound and rhythm relationships, our shared sense of time is bound to the cosmos and to the animal world.

Just as there is a body time within us as part of cosmic time and infinity, so there is also a body space upon earth within the infinitude of sky space. A child's first discovery of balance on two legs is a wonder to observe. The fear of losing that assured balance is one of the most painful aspects of aging. With erectness, humankind established for the species a new place, a new space in the world. The thigh muscles must have become slowly strong and coordinated enough over time in order to support and balance a two-legged wingless animal with free arms and hands. The wonder of this achievement is revealed to us when the toddler demonstrates this process for us in slow motion.

From this posture, human beings derived the flexibility of spine and neck and the extension of arms and legs, which reaches its highest art form in dance and gives a sense of body space unique in the animal world. This we share with all other human beings, as we also share the infinitude of the sky and the boundless stretches of great open spaces of which we are aware even though they may not be part of our immediate geographical setting.

But, again, the variety of space boundaries within which individuals are forced to live is idiosyncratic and leaves its mark on the body-space relationships of each person. Space limitations may be inhibiting or may prove to stimulate great inventiveness and dexterity. Too wide a wide-open area might make a human being feel very small or suggest an ungrounded sensation of floating off into infinity.

Just as human beings have developed through the ages an ultimate form of expression unique to each sense, so also these arts have evolved *form,* an organic integrity which superordinates energy, process, and product, eliciting perfection in the whole or, one might say, an integrating power which synthesizes organically.

The word *form* has taken on so many usages in our language that it serves us well to sort them out in order better to employ this term. When we are discussing it in relation to art it is important to remember that it has two aspects. Some of the usages, which have a derogatory bite when employed, alert us to possible flaws which may appear in a work of art that is not integrated or not organic. We speak of things, or events, as being "too formal" or representing "empty form." There can be "show without substance" or "mere form." There is a suspicion sometimes of "slavish conforming"; an excessive emphasis on mere originality may deteriorate into a "uniform," meaningless "conformity."

All the arts embrace some set forms or designations of pattern or schema. Poems have been classified, for example, into explicit forms such as sonnets, odes, and epics, as well as open modern forms. Music, also, uses the word *form* to designate a set or prescribed order, such as the sonata or opera form. But regardless of how perfectly the form has been adhered to, the intrinsic form within that form must not be "empty" or "mere" or "meaningless" if it is to have the authority, the integrity, of art.

The dictionary gives us a definition which is useful: Form means "the organization and placement of basic elements to show relationship and produce a coherent image." Another definition states that it is "the formal structure of a work of art." Well and good. But I submit that when artists discuss form with one another or in their work with students, they refer to some more basic, essential quality. This quality is that which binds us all to nature, to all organic phenomena, and is integrating. The bond remains, although as artists we must somehow strive to transcend with inspiration where we cannot surpass with skill.

The precepts by which connoiseurs appraise a work of art may be variously formulated. However, they will probably include such phrases as "organic structure" and "living form." Active words define the way the lines run, the pattern spreads, the space is enclosed, and how the whole "hangs together." These phrases are naturally appropriate for all the performing arts. However, they also serve the graphic arts. The painting in the process of becoming is alive, taking form. It must remain alive when finished, so balanced and vital that in it one sees a living form, a perfect instant of growth. With frames we capture such works for they promise to forever re-enliven us by their presence.

Windows were called "wind-eyes" in long-ago England and sometimes were even circular, the eyes of the wall. Through these eyes the inhabitants of a building received light and took in the lively outdoor scene, which offered a constant pattern of changes. The artist is challenged to catch and hold this in all its vitality and preserve it within these molding strictures of time and space and organic growth—form.

Is it not the restoring function of paintings, these "wind-eyes" breaking through blank walls, to bring us back to our senses?

Each art offers its own formal approach for the serious student. What the child must learn about matter and sound and movement through sensory perception and much trial and error, the young would-be artist must recapture in an atmosphere which elicits creative activity and be guided by those accomplished in the art to be pursued.

Each field involves unending study, training, and practice. Out of all this concentrated effort the discipline of the art is matured. We speak often of this discipline and, indeed, it is a mandatory element wherever art experience is pursued. But it is not clear to many people what is involved in this learning process, why it is of such importance, or, indeed, what its limitations are. For years of study and training, however rigorous, cannot produce an artist.

Only processes and skills can be taught. The most gifted teacher can only free the creative impulse, the creative drive, and these only sometimes, in another person. The teacher who is also a professional artist and consistently works in a dedicated way with a chosen medium can emanate to others his devotion to this activity. Sometimes such a teacher will activate in others the deep need to recapture those moments in childhood when, enabled to grasp the vibrantly colored threads of each perceptive experience, she may weave them into a meaningful wholeness—a new form. This accomplishment brings with it a sense of great power, for then the child or adult is both maker and creator, and in harmony with all the forces of nature.

# 3

# The Woven
# Life Cycle

The psychosocial theory of the human life cycle was presented at the White House Conference on Infancy and Childhood by Erik and Joan Erikson in Washington, D.C., in 1950.* It is based on the premise that eight basic strengths emerge as we go through life, each the outgrowth of a time-specific developmental confrontation. It is therefore an epigenetic theory. It takes into consideration psychological, social, and biological constraints and the supports of the environment, the whole matrix in which the individual grows.

Epigenesis is the theory that traces the development of the embryo according to a biological time pattern in a mandatory sequence. This sequential growth, as noted in

---

*Transactions of the Fourth Conference on Infancy and Childhood.*
New York: Josiah Macy, Jr., Foundation, 1950.

the first chapter, is now known to be more influenced by the social milieu than was in previous years considered possible. The sequence, still, maintains and this holds true also for the life-cycle theory. However, according to the life-cycle theory, the influence of the societal matrix in all its environmental aspects plays a more tangible and conspicuous role in post-uteral development. Where a strength is not adequately developed according to the given sequence for its scheduled period of critical resolution, the supports of the environment may bring it into appropriate balance at a later period. Hope remains constant throughout life that more sturdy resolutions of the basic confrontation may be realized.

The accompanying chart resembles a two-dimensional scaffold (Chart 1). What is important about this depiction is that it suggests movement, progress, steps, and ultimately destination, in this case, a sense of wisdom. Wisdom is accrued through experienced knowledge verified by acute senses.

It should be stated from the onset that throughout this presentation the role of the senses and artistic creativity at the various stages of the life cycle will be stressed. This emphasis stems from the conviction that, in all schooling and in the social order in general, cognition and the measurable aspects of scientific enterprise are overstressed. The resulting underestimation of playful imagination, inventiveness, can lead to a regimentation of "facts," often based on half-truths, which dominate thinking and planning. Growth, resiliency, and creativity all suffer. A technological world could be both dull and dangerous.

Now let us look at this same black-and-white chart produced as a weaving, in order to guide our *senses* as well as our comprehension by means of texture, context, and color (Chart 2).

CHART 1. Eight Stages of Psychosocial Development of the Human Life Cycle

| | 1 | 2 | 3 | 4 | 5 | 6 | 7 | 8 |
|---|---|---|---|---|---|---|---|---|
| Old Age | | | | | | | | Integrity vs. Despair. WISDOM |
| Adulthood | | | | | | | Generativity vs. Stagnation. CARE | |
| Young Adulthood | | | | | | Intimacy vs. Isolation. LOVE | | |
| Adolescence | | | | | **Identity vs. Role** Confusion. FIDELITY | | | |
| School Age | | | | Industry vs. Inadequacy. COMPETENCE | | | | |
| Play Age | | | Initiative vs. Guilt. PURPOSE | | | | | |
| Early Childhood | | Autonomy vs. Shame, Doubt. WILL | | | | | | |
| Infancy | Basic Trust vs. Basic Mistrust. HOPE | | | | | | | |

At the bottom of the weaving are the loose threads of the warp. Eight colors depict the basic strengths and the critical stage at which they should become firm and strong. An equal number of gray threads are present to modify appropriately the surge of colors and to represent the opposite, conflicting elements. The *dark blue* threads represent basic *trust,* and the *gray* ones with which they are intertwined *basic mistrust.* The strength to be developed, as the black-and-white chart indicates, is *hope.* We have designated *trust* the syntonic element, and *mistrust* the dystonic. The tension between these two poles is constant throughout the life cycle, and indeed, the life cycle is as taut with tension as the warp itself, stretched vertically on the loom in the process of being woven. On the loom, however, the tension is constant, while life's tensions are more random, if predictable—at least for the developmental stages.

A resolution of the balance between the syntonic and dystonic poles is a consistent demand for everyone throughout the life cycle. No permanent achievement of a firm balance is possible while the unpredictable vicissitudes of life, with all its changes, continue. Every new element in the social matrix can modify the tension one way or the other. Constant rebalancing of earlier stages and encounters unsatisfactorily balanced are then to be faced and refaced throughout life. There is no firm ground. It is a continuous process. However, with luck, determination, or grace, strengths increase and become more staunch and dependable. The elements of the looked-for wisdom can accrue to guide and encourage.

The warp itself is the framework, the consistent element of support. The strengths are there and have been since before birth, as the lower fringe of the weaving indicates. No resolution is final in the ongoing pulls between syntonic and dystonic elements, but opportunities to change strategies and patterns are constant. Trust and hope, for example, may be difficult to maintain because much mistrust is reasonable. But they are given potential in the warp, and are developed to some degree in infancy. They have survived and can be nurtured, encouraged, and strengthened.

So we begin with dark blue for basic trust (syntonic) to be balanced by the gray basic mistrust (dystonic). The other warp colors are:

Orange for will, with autonomy (syntonic) as opposed to gray shame and doubt (dystonic).

Dark green for purpose, with initiative and its opposite, gray guilt.

Yellow for competence, its contraries being industry and inadequacy, gray.

Light blue for fidelity, with identity pulling against role confusion, gray.

Rosy red for love, with intimacy and its opposite gray pole, isolation.

Light green for care, with generativity juxtaposed with dull self-abjugation and stagnation.

Purple for wisdom, with integrity and its polar opposite, gray disintegrating despair.

At this point I would like to add a personal note. As mentioned earlier, my husband and I together prepared the chart and the description of the eight stages. The theory was further elaborated and evolved in a number of his books in the following years. Naturally I believed that I understood it completely in all of its ramifications. Actually I never really thoroughly *grasped* all its implications until I rather playfully undertook the process of setting up a warp of eight colors and began to see the blending of these colors as my fingers guided threads of identical color through the warp. The threads themselves had duplicated the black-and-white chart—but in color. For the first time my mind and senses collaborated and made the idea manifest. I understood; I knew. Moreover, those empty boxes of the black-and-white chart werenow literally full of meaning. What does that blue of trust do to the orange of autonomy, coupled with the gray of shame and doubt? I see supporting blue lines of hope in that second lower-left-hand square. In the top line of the final weaving, observe how all the early strengths present themselves, bolstering the purple stage of aging.

I took special pleasure in the lower fringe of colored threads as they hung loose and unformed, for they represent the potential strengths as they are present and promised to the neonate in utero—perhaps even in the genes. And I enjoy the drooping fringe threads at the top since they suggest continuation, generationally speaking, and promise in an unknown. I have referred to this upper cluster of threads as the "unknown fringe benefits."

This is the kind of laborious process from which one learns immeasurably. Having carried out a rough sample to demonstrate the validity of the plan, I realized how complicated and meticulous the skills must become in order to perfect such a project. I looked for and found a skilled and experienced weaver, Mary Schoenbrun, who could teach and guide me and finally execute the finished weaving.

Let me now introduce a second idea and a new weaving (Chart 3). All the stages with their strengths and syntonic and dystonic elements are presented in the first two charts as filling a similar space of time. This time space is not in accord with actuality. Infancy is short, lasting only about one and a half years. Adulthood is long, perhaps thirty or more years, and the span of old age has, in time, become increasingly longer. Human development is idiocentric, though certainly governed throughout by physical epigenesis (integration) and slow but inevitable disintegration. No exact time schedule for any stage has been designated, but they are represented in the developmental progression in which they are related to one another.

In order to comprehend the life cycle cognitively and perceptually, this time element is indicated in the third chart.

Now I would like to introduce you to this weaving process and share with you some of the insights which rewarded me when, for the first time, the woven interrelationships of the colored threads became actual. Bear with the process, which may seem somewhat pedantic. In fact, put yourself into it, if possible, by imagining that these experiences with the syntonic and dystonic opposites are the tugs and pushes of your own stages and years, or those of your children. Where you remember more grayness, more dystonic elements at a stage in the woof, imagine it there; when the memories glow, increase the brilliance of the color in your mind's eye. You may remember a great deal as you weave. Let me remind you that not only women have been weavers. In other lands weaving is the work of men, and they are masters of their craft. Following the steps, weaving in the new stages, is a challenge which I recommend for the artist in each of us. It can be a rewarding experience. Incidentally, now that we have shared an "experienced" conceptual clarification, we can claim that all conceptualization proceeds according to a similar interweaving of sensory and conceptual processes.

CHART 3

CHART 2

CHART 4

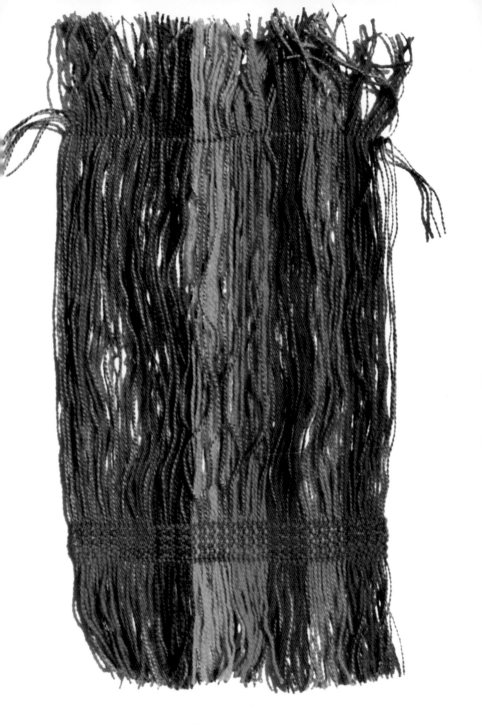

CHART 5

CHART 6

CHART 7

CHART 8

CHART 9

CHART 10

Let us begin our woven chart by introducing our first blue threads across the warp and observing the mingling of colors, while at the same time maintaining a consistent tensile strength in the stretched threads (Chart 4). As we shift the treadle and shuttle the thread back to the left, we see a new pattern form, and the blending of the other colors with the blue becomes more observable. We will proceed in this manner until four threads have been stretched across—a short space indeed on this large warp, just as infancy comprises only a fraction (but what a fraction) of the "average expectable" human life cycle.

## Blue—HOPE:
## Basic Trust vs. Basic Mistrust

The first stage is woven with the blue thread of infancy. The strength to be fostered is a firm sense of *hope*, which can only emerge from the favorable balance of a pair of opposites: *basic trust* and *basic mistrust*. Such a pair I consider "necessary contraries," for life can only be faced with a potentially trusting outlook, and yet cannot be lived without some adaptive mistrust to ensure survival. Nor are we ever free of these confrontations, which continue in the form of inner stresses throughout life.

The newborn organism is a bundle of senses and sensations which have slowly been developing in utero, forming a one-of-a-kind human child. This small being has butted its way head first into an alien environment and has begun to respond to innumerable signals. Warmth, the touch of skin, modulated sounds are undoubtedly reassuring; other sensations may be offensive, and the sounds the breath and throat produce in protest originate startlingly close to the ear. Both *receptivity* and *protest* are vital reactions. Infants must learn to trust their senses, for they are dependent on them for life itself. They perceive, comprehend with all the senses, and the information received must be trustworthy.

When, however, the sensory stimuli are overcharged—the light is too glaring, the sound too sudden or too loud, the food too thick or too bitter—there must be a defensive reaction of protest. A struggle then ensues between the need to see, hear, or appease the hunger and the dissatisfaction caused by the inappropriateness of the stimuli offered. We look to the parents to keep the environment adequately satisfying and judiciously controlled. In such a setting, the inevitable pull between trusting recep tivity and mistrusting protest remains constant, although it can be resolved in periods of contentment and rest.

Children who are too trusting or too passively expectant may not develop the initiative necessary to demand attention based on genuine need. Too much protest can deprive the mistrustful one of well-meant offerings. It remains essential throughout life to learn to perceive and accurately judge the appropriateness of our reactions, which form the basis for good common sense and later on for seasoned wisdom. Perceptiveness, then, as we have pointed out, is the sum of sensory knowledge as it is stored, synthesized, and accumulated in the brain cells. Those oversized heads that make it so difficult for a child to enter the world seem barely adequate for the processing and storing which our slow (human) development demands.

We have not spoken yet of the impact of human relationships on the newborn child, but the eagerness or reluctance with which the infant is received into its enviornment charges the atmosphere in which the first breath is taken. Here the generational sequence makes itself felt, for to be greeted with a heartfelt yes can certainly tip the scale toward a positive sense of well-being.

In turn, the infant comes into the world, as described above, with all sensory modalities prepared for functioning and ready for mutuality.

There has been, and continues to be, a diversity of opinion as to when infants sense themselves to be separate entities. Lacking definitive data to hold to, perceptions based on accumulated experience must serve. I believe that this moment is signified by the meeting of the eyes—probably the mother's eyes—with the infant's, and the early responses to this experience. The eye effort made by the baby to really focus, to truly see, is touching indeed. After success follows, the smile engendered is moving beyond words. Contact has been made. The other has been identified. A relationship eye to eye—I to I— has been validated. It is with the eyes that concern and love are communicated, and distance and anger as well. Growing maturity does not alter this basic connection, for all through life our communication with others is eye centered. However, as described earlier, when eyes fail the other senses compensate with increased acuity, and hearing and touch may form the communication.

Initially, then, one must know and trust oneself in order to be able to perceive when to be trusting and when to mistrust. The information on which perceptiveness is based will be only as accurate as the senses are sharp and reliable. Stored sensory experience will suggest acceptance or refusal, receptivity or protest. The struggle may be resolved affirmatively or negatively, depending on the trust which has been engendered through the years by the caring persons who tend to the needs of the infant. Where dependable mutuality has developed, there will be a trustworthy communication which goes far toward establishing the vital strengths: for the infant, trustfulness; and for the adult caring person, the reciprocal strength of care.

In the course of every life the challenges and obstacles that time inevitably introduces are unending, as is the need for a constant rebalancing of trusting receptivity and mistrustful protest. Even without the traumas of misadventure and loss, life is extraordinarily difficult. When traumas occur, there is inevitably a temporary imbalance, a letdown toward depression and anxiety.

Through the centuries those who care for infants have known that lullabies quiet and console, soft rhythmic patting or rocking soothes, and bright, moving visual stimuli will distract and placate an unhappy baby—all of which establish rudimentary sensory modes for potential forms of expression.

### Hope and Will: Blue and Orange
### (Autonomy vs. Shame and Doubt)

To the right of the all-blue square where the blue of trust and hope is most clear, we can see how the bright orange warp representing *will* has begun to be woven into the blueness of the first stage and how the gray of shame and doubt modifies both the blue and the orange threads. The warp, we suggest, is intended to indicate the source, the early vestiges of the vital strengths which we will follow as they develop through the life cycle. Is there rudimentary evidence of willpower in the behavior of the infant?

In swaddling and in overrestrictive diapering or covering, doubt and frustration may be induced by the limiting of kinesthetic autonomy. These periods of frustration, however, are followed by the release of restriction during bathing and changing of clothing. This allows a satisfying alternation, but it also emphasizes the helplessness of the infant during periods of restriction. Perhaps deprivation of movement may tend to focus the senses on observation and listening, sharpening these senses. Some appropriate alternation of both must be established to ensure a developing sense of autonomy and of support and protection. It is true that the swaddled baby often is allowed an upright position so that the eyes can follow what goes on all around. A cradled or cribbed infant may see only the ceiling, which is neither stimulating nor entertaining, and in our culture this could entail real visual deprivation. Might such deprivation also induce regular explosions of kinesthetic energy and great hunger for tactile and visual satisfaction, such as has been noted in swaddled babies in Russia and in American Indian settings? The kinetic energy of infants varies distinctly, as do cultural mores, and so we do not know how to offer control and freedom to the maximum benefit of each child.

*Hope and Purpose: Blue and Dark Green*
*(Initiative vs. Guilt)*

Early vestiges of inventiveness and initiative are displayed by even a very young infant. They are represented in the weaving by the dark green threads. Active nuzzling and groping for the mother's breast, stimulated by a well-developed sense of smell, are innate abilities of the newborn. Later, reaching for objects and the manipulation involved in bringing a blanket or toy to the mouth for sensitive investigation stimulate real inventiveness. Perhaps most delightfully audible are the sounds an infant makes both for sheer satisfaction and for getting attention, a whole repertoire that can include bubble blowing, gurgling, squealing, singing, the wail of complaint, and finally the screams of exasperated fury.

## Hope and Competence: Blue and Yellow
## (Industry vs. Inadequacy)

As these improvisations are found satisfactory and pursued, a certain competent coordination of musculature develops. Sucking becomes more efficient; solid foods can be manipulated and later conveyed to the mouth by hand. Biting comes with newly formed teeth. In fact, the degree of development of control of both small and large muscle groups which evolves during this first year of life is astonishing. The lively yellow threads in the warp represent such early competencies, conspicuously adding their vital strength to this fourth rectangle.

However, if the infant's greedy need for stimulus and companionship interferes with the mother's needs or those of other siblings, her facial response to a demanding call may clearly show annoyance. Having evoked this displeasure the child may experience a rudimentary sense of guilt. Very early sharing must also be part of the learning of this period. Again there are hazards. If parents are oversolicitous and enjoy the dependencies of the baby too much, the opportunities for developing skills may be restricted. On the other hand, if too little sensory stimulation is offered, the senses remain dull or undeveloped.

## Hope and Fidelity: Dark Blue and Light Blue
## (Identity vs. Role Confusion)

To an inattentive eye all babies may look alike, but newborn babies are, in fact, more apt to look like old men and women just recovering from a difficult sea voyage. Each one looks unique, and to the careful observer, the newness—the specialness—is clearly apparent. The blue threads in the fifth rectangle mark what may later be made into a very personal sense of identity. It is the province of the whole family, including aunts, uncles, and friends, to make the newcomer feel special and unique within the boundaries of good sense.

### *Hope and Love: Blue and Red*
### *(Intimacy vs. Isolation)*

The rosy red threads in the neighboring rectangle suggest the early roots of what will become intimacy, closeness, love. Surely the physical contact with the mother and the warm mutuality of their relationship must be the precursor of deep affection and also passion. In our day fathers are becoming equally essential figures from the earliest contact. Where such nurturance is altogether lacking, no amount of sterile care suffices to induce age-specific development. In infancy the overriding need for closeness, for stimulation through skin contact, is critical. In utero the neonate's entire surface is surrounded by warm, moving amniotic fluid. Deprivation of this stimulus with inadequate compensation from caretakers can result in the onset of the sense of isolation, a dulling of intimacy.

### *Hope and Care: Blue and Light Green*
### *(Generativity vs. Stagnation)*

The incorporation of the images of those benevolent persons who hover over the earliest, neediest period of one's life is mandatory for all productivity and creativity. The development of this strength, this quality of "caring for," is the generational task for species survival. Where the rudiments of caring have not been part of the learning experience of the infant, later relationships may be difficult or unfeeling.

*Hope and Wisdom: Blue and Purple*
*(Integrity vs. Despair)*

Following the green threads of generativity are the purple ones denoting *wisdom* and *integrity*. Even in their most subtle, vestigial sense, these are big words to apply to an infant. But has it not been noted repeatedly how carefully a baby studies the face of a stranger? This integrity, as yet free from the strictures of social response, is the infant's birthright. But we cannot ignore the impression that the needy cry of a baby in distress, unattended, alone, is the cry of genuine *despair*.

A tacit understanding, an innate perceptiveness of what is trustworthy in the offered relationship seems often to be sensed. Before set social responses have been conveyed, the baby is still free to judge with the innocent eye and ear of the as yet uninitiated—with his or her whole being.

## Orange—WILL:
## Autonomy vs. Shame and Doubt (Chart 5)

The orange thread launches the second stage, in which toddlers find themselves newly in command of their musculature and eager to investigate their world, try out their capacities, and exercise their will. A critical confrontation ensues between *autonomy* and the *shame* and *doubt* which plague these little persons as they go too far, fail, or are reprimanded.

Throughout infancy, the musculature has been increasing in tone and strength. Movement for sheer kinesthetic pleasure becomes a component of every waking moment—movement for exploration or for the developing urges to reach, to pull, to crawl. The acuteness of all the senses is coordinated into kinetic behavior, offering direction, balance, and tactile security, stimulated by smell and taste.

When the youngster is beginning to stand, or even as crawling is perfected, a new phase of learning begins that opens up wide possibilities as well as innumerable restrictions. Anthropologists have been amazed at the freedom allowed tiny children in the "primitive" natural settings where they live. Depending on the specific demands of their environment and cultural milieu, they are confidently permitted to handle sharp tools and climb steep rocks. They learn their own limitations early and increase their skills in mastering the environment with the help of an extended family and older children.

In Western technological society, there are innumerable restrictions for toddlers, many realistic, others more indicative of the anxiety of caretaking adults. With the child's constant testing of limits, tensions are set up, and these are too often dictated by the mood swings of adults rather than by actual danger. Adults are inconsistent, arousing expectations which remain unfulfilled and making careless promises. They are often as unconscious of the limitations they needlessly impose on children as they are of the fact that their own fears and anxieties were probably generated in their childhoods.

To be curious, adventurous, willing, and even eager to experiment are all qualities we recognize as being essential to the creative process. Obviously, if these are restricted or discouraged through the regular expression of doubt in the child's capacities, they will be repressed, thereby limiting the information which the senses are so ready to garner and store. Parental anxiety, too, is contagious and can inhibit many an adventurous impulse.

What a freedom the toddler can discover in the world of things (pots, pans, toys, blocks, dolls) and of materials (sand, water, toy clay, paper). They offer a concrete directness, never deceiving, exploiting, shaming, or doubting either motives or capacities. In complete silence they inform and allow the child to practice skills and to perfect coordinations. The signals they give are unequivocably clear and consistent. Materials are the law-abiding elements of earth, and in their integrity is silent strength.

Making with materials is, of course, the essence of the art process. At no time in life is the human organism more ready for this opening up into the world of materials. The senses are eager for information, for experience. The musculature is hungry for action and bent on expressing every kinesthetic impulse. Leeway for this adventurous drive is necessary, as is also a judicious curbing through the aware use of the senses so that danger can be perceived and not merely verbalized. Sensible denials are more acceptable if they have been preceded by an earlier base of mutual trust. But life without many resounding yes responses would be a dull ordeal. Through this period, then, one learns to will what is sensible and pleasurable, indeed what the senses have taught.

I will not now proceed, as with the first stage of trust vs. mistrust, to discuss the merging of orange with all the other stages and their colors. This can be undertaken by each reader individually, not neglecting to blend in an appropriate share of gray shame and doubt.

## Dark Green—PURPOSE:
## Initiative vs. Guilt (Chart 6)

In the play age which follows, the youngster pursues her activities with a developing purposefulness, and green denotes this third strength. With increasing freedom of movement the child mobilizes heightened initiative both in action and in imagination, which is, however, confronted by a sense of guilt when the boundaries posed by other people's space, feelings, and things are disregarded.

With the mastery of the musculature demonstrated by the ability to walk, run, and dance, and with the coordination necessary for making and doing with materials, the youngster is ready for serious play, imaginative play. If a realistic sense of trust is in control and will is getting both strong and flexible, imagination can now flourish and make all things possible.

Playing roles comes so naturally to young children at this stage, improvising relationships with things and materials, and trying out "being" whomever or whatever their imaginations devise. The importance of this play is immeasurable. To act the part of someone else is stretching, evoking both empathy and self-knowledge. Group activities bring the awareness that others have wills, purposes, and competencies which must be considered and dealt with—or the game is off. The skills of group interrelationships need to be learned early.

This is the time for delight in body movement just for sheer pleasure, for experimenting with sounds, composing songs and melodies of one's own, dramatizing one's own imaginative scenarios, playing with words, and claiming one's own personal vocabulary. With accruing competence, the child is now ready to carry out the schemes a lively imagination proposes, with all available materials. It is a wonderful world. Curiosity, invention, abounding vitality, and enthusiasm make this stage of growth one to be supported and nourished, and never quite forgotten or relinquished.

The activities which have been described briefly may sound so unstructured that a formless education comes to mind. Quite the opposite is true, for the media of the arts require innate disciplines, and the artist-teacher who has mastered a chosen art form must pass on this grounded knowledge of artistic practice and its formal processes and demands.

Once again both inner and outer limitations are mandatory. Guilt can be induced in the child if in sudden anger (in fantasy or in reality) he destroys whatever or whoever is causing his frustration—for those very things and people are also beloved and needed. In actual play, also, this enthusiastic spontaneity must be bounded by the needs and rights of others.

From the warp fringes where the vital strengths dangle their roots we can trace what the other colors are offering to enhance this lively stage of initiative.

The potential of competence is increasing rapidly, identity is already sensed in uniqueness, friendships offer an early sense of intimacy, and all types of caring for people and things is constantly exercised—wisdom continues to accrue.

## Yellow—COMPETENCE:
### Industry vs. Inadequacy

The school age, in which all cultures teach their young the skills necessary to cope in their social milieu, is woven in yellow. The sense of *competence* is the strength to be developed. Learning demands *industry,* and the counter pull to be dealt with is a sense of inferiority, of *inadequacy.*

One special reason the imagination must be consistently fostered during the play age is because it is in this school-age stage, which follows it, that one must learn the basic skills. The great danger in putting heavy emphasis on skills without having first developed sensitivity, playfulness, and imagination is that the end product may be mere virtuosity. It is the function of the school age, the age of learning in all societies, to develop the fourth vital strength, a sense of competence. Without it, a sense of inferiority may limit the development of capacities. We can assume that competence must inevitably include discipline, without which one cannot do anything well. Where curiosity has been supported earlier, the child may successfully become involved enough to experience the satisfaction of persisting purposefully. But discipline, which is needed for the development of excellence, is never very attractive in its own right. However, there isn't any known way to dodge it. Where motivation is high, it becomes less onerous; every artist, draftsman, and creative worker knows that without it one does not become skillful and competent.

The hitch is that without competence and the skills that society respects, the young person is apt to feel ineffective, useless, or discouraged. Unfortunately, our preoccupation with spectator sports, with television, and with the media now often preempts the time formerly used in learning skills of participation, rather than passive observation. These "pass-times" such as television do not even stimulate the imagination. They just take over and do it all for us, leaving a youngster with illusions of grandeur and no competence to get there. And when these false stimuli are unavailable, those who have become dependent on them tend to feel empty, hollow, incompetent, and inadequate. Since a child's senses vary in acuity according to genetic endowment and to the nurturing environment in which they have developed, we must expect competencies to vary as well. Environments, families, communities, and cultures hold priorities which promote what they most need and respect. Whereas, for example, the American Indians held it to be of paramount importance to know and live in skillful harmony with their natural environment, in our culture we tend to promote book learning, calculation, and technical cleverness—no matter where children live.

It is possible to argue persuasively that those competencies which are basic to artistic expression are those which also support cognitive development. This is not just a belief, since a number of studies have now backed up this contention.* It has also been repeatedly noted that during the school years the spontaneous, freely inventive quality of a child's artwork becomes dull. The school years, spent as they are in learning the necessary conformity to the society one lives in, are also devoted to curricula planned to progress stepwise toward set graduation goals. This involves competition and the memorizing of facts, figures, and multiplication tables through relentless discipline. Process-oriented art experience does not flourish in such an atmosphere. Although some schools do incorporate the arts into the curriculum, even the freest programs are bound by city, state, and college requirements for the higher rungs of the educational ladder.

Experiments and pilot studies have been undertaken to incorporate the arts more realistically into school programs, and some of these have had notable success: the Alvarado Project in San Francisco, for example, made funds available to introduce professional artists into schools. Their presence and performance had a truly leavening effect on the vital involvement of students as manifested not only in their artwork but also by the regularity of their attendance at school. The lively murals and finely crafted pottery, woodwork, and textiles that were produced through this program offered clear evi-

*See Rockefeller Report, *Coming to Our States*. New York: McGraw-Hill, 1977.

94

dence that art can flourish in the public school system. Currently, in San Francisco, an organization called LEAP (Learning through Education in the Arts Project) is placing artists of all disciplines in public school classrooms to create with the children. The whole curriculum becomes alive when cognitive material is imaginatively transformed into art forms.

Where family households place a high value on art expression and maintain an atmosphere conducive to active participation in making and doing, music, dance, and poetry, these arts may continue to grow. In a society where the outer appearance of a room is more important than what takes place there, a child will not have the space or flexibility necessary to experiment with tools and materials and to make order later. Overemphasis on orderliness and cleanliness inhibits play and teaches a static sense of pride in ownership rather than in active engagement.

We have postulated that some modicum of competence is necessary just for survival. Challenging situations, and change itself, demand great ingeniousness plus skill and coordination. Since we are unable to really plan for a preordained future, a wider range for initiative and competence seems more than desirable in the school years.

## Light Blue—FIDELITY:
## Identity vs. Role Confusion (Chart 8)

In the early work years or continued education of young people, a sense of fidelity to oneself and to one's own values to co-workers, associates, and ideologies is the strength to be fostered. For this to be even temporarily experienced, a unique sense of personal identity, for which we use pale blue thread, must emerge. The contrary pull is to avoid any commitment and to remain with a confusion, a fragmentation, of identity components.

Provided the strengths of the earlier stages are staunch, this is the time when a young person may emerge as a unique individual with a sense of pride and trust in unique capacities and a sense of active competence with which a personal environment can be shaped or reshaped.

Our chart indicates clearly that the young person is now at a crossroad, the great divide between childhood—the school years—and adult life. Even a tentative resolution of the pulls and pressures between a personal sense of identity and the indecisions of identity confusion may take many years of struggle, or it may occur suddenly in a moment of clarity. The conviction about who you are may come about like a revelation, like a wise interpretation. But there are also those whose struggle is long and painful, who make many false starts and are forced to change direction all too often. But life demands at this point that commitments be made and directions be chosen. In a culture which is as specialized as our own, the choice of one route may often exclude others.

We are postulating that to have emerged from childhood with a sense of basic trust in one's own senses, in the world and in one's fellow men and women is the first premise for vital growth.. At this crossroad, the young adult, emerging from high school or apprenticeship, faces the challenge of self-trust, trust in a personal "I" that can be related to the social matrix and its ideological stance. Decisions are necessary at this stage, not only concerning what and who one is to be within the social milieu, but also about what ideas and convictions one will stand up for and defend with loyalty and fidelity. That this becoming is charged with struggle and tension is an understatement.

9 6

## Red—LOVE:
## Intimacy vs. Isolation (Chart 9)

Early adulthood is the stage for the development of mature *love*. For this sixth strength we have used red. *Intimacy*, a true closeness and sharing, becomes possible and, indeed, deeply needed. Loving sexual intimacy includes giving and receiving, and assumes responsibility. The contrary pull is toward uninvolvement and isolation.

So far, our focus has been on the individual, with little reference to those others with whom the life space is shared. Initially, of course, this is usually the family and later includes neighbors, school friends, and the community in an ever-widening circle. Beyond the family, as time goes on, selectivity begins and personal ties are formed: sharing of mutual interests, of secrets, of intimacies with chosen others. Sometimes the friendships endure, but it is as likely that time and change will alter circumstances so that, though many friends and acquaintants will remain, there will be only a few deeply intimate and lasting relationships.

This is the first of the three adult stages, and it may be well to review at this point the prerequisite of the most essential of the strengths, namely, love.

Let us assume that optimal balance between basic trust and basic mistrust can be maintained; that autonomy and initiative are resilient but bridled by sensible judgment and respect for others; and that competence is adequate to offset inevitable inadequacies. One must hope especially that identity and fidelity are strong enough at this point to permit an adult experience of "finding oneself as one loses oneself in another"—as one does when love is mutual.

It is for this reason that, regardless of previous intimacies, trivial or deeply meaningful as they may have been, the young adult is first ready for an experience that involves commitment and fidelity capable of culminating in mature love. This presupposes the sharing of life, work, and productivity nurtured by the bond of adult sexuality and a sense of common goals and even of ideologies. It therefore demands two already defined identities, neither of which becomes really submerged under the dominance of the other, although each may be both modified and expanded.

Clearly love does not first emerge at this stage of the life cycle. Each previous stage has been colored in our weaving by the red threads which are present in the very fringes of the warp. The infant's dependent but delighted attachment to parents, the toddler's assurance of a physical welcoming following forays into independence, and the sensual pleasure of cuddling and caring for animals and soft toys have supported intimacy at their given stages. Friends have offered and received affection, and there have been the other more intimate relationships of adolescence.

Where these precursors of adult love have been lacking and expression of affection limited, the young adult otherwise so ready to become a partner in a "we" relationship will resort to disengagement and find solace in solitude.

Perhaps at this point, as we focus our attention on the first adult stage and such a vital strength as love, we should consider more realistically the devastation possibly left by inconclusive encounters and debilitating confrontations with the gray dystonic. So far, our weaving has emphasized the bright colors of the strengths which we have presupposed to be present as a resolution, however tentative, to each crisis. There has been no gray woven into the woof. But the average life is not possible without gray experiences—the misadventures and losses that add to the odds against the struggle for positive balance. Imbalance can, of course, be offset by a variety of interventions, but if from the beginning of life the level of mistrust has been so high that one cannot risk any receiving, all interventions and offerings will be unacceptable. A negativistic reaction pattern has been set up. Once again we should stress the importance of the struggles for balance as a strengthening process. The strongest and best among us are those who have overcome challenging obstacles with sometimes desperate determination. However, years of work with young emotionally disturbed patients have taught us that where hope, will, purpose, and competence are unsteady, identity and love are difficult to establish.

There may be vestiges of intimacy in all this dreary development. There must be, for the rosy red threads continue to climb the weaving. In fact, one should contend that exactly these threads are a kind of lifeline for every individual, since if any intervention can break the dullness of the graying pattern, it will be the experience of an intimate relationship. Only by means of such a genuine mutuality can empathy slowly retrieve some of the lost vitality of the insecure basic strengths.

## Light Green—CARE:
### Generativity vs. Stagnation (Chart 10)

At this point in the life cycle the individual may be less than thirty years old. There follows a span of approximately thirty-five years of adulthood in which to take *care* of the young, of one's work, and of the community. This is the stage of *generativity* (woven in green), of generating in every sense of the word—procreativity, productivity, creativity—through an investment of one's capacities in the well-being of the generations to follow, and concern for the elders who have preceded. Such commitment places heavy responsibilities, but withdrawal—which is the counter pull—is to retreat into a kind of *stagnation.*

The green threads of the wool now begin their long stretch of weaving, the years of generating. At this point in the life cycle the adult is called upon to take part in what the Hindus call "the maintenance of the world." It encompasses a period of many years of responsibilities that demand stamina and dedication. The challenge is to be productive in all manner of ways, and the strength to be developed is that of *care.*

The caring embraces taking care of whatever one produces, children, of course, but also all that one does or makes or of which one is part. The maintenance involves playing an active role in the social institutions which create the coherence of a given social structure at a given historical time. Not to be in any way productive and participant in the social network in which one lives and works and loves must result in stagnation—a sense of the end of growth, both personally and as a member of the community and the greater polis.

This sounds very vague because the diversity of work available and the variety of roles to be played are so extensive that it is quite staggering to consider the opportunities and choices. A look at the charted life cycle indicates very clearly what essentially is demanded of adults in the community during those approximately thirty-five years of the dominance of generativity.

Wherever they are and under whatever conditions, the adults of a given society owe the younger generation the safeguarding of its opportunities, the conditions under which the basic strengths can be developed. They provide the foundation for all future generativity, creativity, and productivity.

We have stressed the importance of proximity and touch between the caregiver and the infant in order to ensure the survival of the infant. Among those who, in turn, nurture the child this closeness and dependence may play an important role in their own existential survival, offering hope for the future as a result of the child's actual presence. Beginning with infancy, let us consider how the social setting organizes and supports the matrix into which the child is born.

Throughout the ages, all cultures, societies, and tribes have sanctioned the intimacies of chosen mates with some form of ritual marriage. The importance of this lies in the establishment of parenthood, in safeguarding the inheritance of titles and material possessions and in assuring generational continuity. At the same time, it provides a stability of relationship which gives the family coherence and secures the development and care of growing children. In such a caring milieu of trustworthy adults, the young child may establish trust and learn to *love*.

Care is the strength of the stage of the "maintenance of the world": caring for and being a participant in all of the social institutions mentioned, and caring about the welfare of others in every sense of the word. When we consider the constancy of change and realize how continually all such organized bodies are in flux, the enormity of the involvement of the adults becomes apparent, for every facet of the social order must be adapted to the historical moment.

As a special province of this generative stage, we find all the caring professions: social welfare, medicine, psychotherapies, and all the associated physical therapies. All require organization and constant supervision, and the area of responsibility is enormous. The adults expressly carry the burden of caring for the young, who are not yet able to fend for themselves, as well as for the old, who are no longer able to function as workers in the social structure.

These are heavy burdens and challenge the highest potential of the strengths garnered from the earlier developmental stages of the life cycle. It is a time, however, when every power is at its height and all goals seem accessible. But should the earlier years have been woven with too many of the gray threads of mistrust, of the shame and doubt in capacities that weaken purpose and will, and if a sense of inferiority has resulted in a feeling of incompetence, promoting confusion about a reasonably sure sense of identity, the brilliance of the green would dull drastically. Such a drab weaving would ensue that we would see the stagnation which the hopeless and defeated feel as they view the activity of the world around them, of which they are such a negligible part.

Needless to say, the losses of this period are many, often drastic—and especially so for those whose life vitality is low. Most certain are the losses of parents, older friends and mentors, and great leaders. Wars bring indescribable losses, and in our time we face the possibility of the ultimate loss, through the use of nuclear weapons and our carelessness regarding the environment, of the planet earth itself.

At the same time, as we all know, these are wonderfully creative years, and change allows new directions and more comprehensive and prudent caring. The awesome truth is that the survival of the culture, even of the species, rests in the hands of the adults of the world. For the overriding burden of the generative years in every culture is the generational future: the maintaining and vitalizing of the basic strengths in the not yet mature segment of the community, and the passing on of such tradition and culture that life may have meaning and value.

## Purple—WISDOM:
## Integrity vs. Despair (Chart 3)

Finally, old age, which is a continually lengthening stage—now twenty or twenty-five years—should show evidence of the accrued strength of wisdom, here woven in purple. Integrity confronts despair in these years that seem to offer more looking back than looking forward. This integrating capacity must be strong enough to offset the physical disintegration that inevitably makes its mark and to endure many losses.

We have reached that age which should culminate in a garnering of the wisdom of the seven previous stages. Shakespeare, then doubtless an arrogant young playwright, described it as the time of the "sere and withered leaf," "sans everything." Probably in the England of that period they had little use for elders, and, in fact, few lived to be old and healthy. But times are changing—and we are changing the times with newly acquired knowledge of how to maintain life and vigor.

We have elected *wisdom* as the word that symbolizes the strength of this last stage of the life cycle and the words *integrity* and *despair* to represent the opposing poles that characterize the tension in the psyche. "Integrity" seems to describe the aging individual's struggles to integrate the strength and purpose necessary to maintain wholeness despite disintegrating physical capacities. It also suggests the need to gather the experiences of a long and eventful life into a meaningful pattern. Old age is a time for remembering and weaving together many disparate elements, and for integrating these incongruities into a comprehensible whole. This integrating has been going on throughout the life cycle, especially as each crisis is faced and the process of resolution itself generates strength. In the same way, despair has been an ingredient of every struggle for balance between the syntonic and dystonic pulls of all stages. But what is wisdom and how can we define its components?

Oddly enough, one finds oneself reaching back into childhood, into beginnings, in order to describe the essentials of wisdom: And through the ages has not childlikeness always been an attribute of the old and wise? With the ripening of age, much learning brings with it quite naturally a genuinely humble curiosity, the return of the "not-knowingness" of the child.

It is affirming to observe how those who have aged with a certain physical integrity are capable of enjoying sensory pleasures with even greater intensity: the sun and the breeze, the fire and the hot drink, the touching of things and people, the parade and the music.

We think of wisdom, too, as that integration of what goes on in the right and left sides of the brain—of the properties of logical functioning combined with the imaginative, spontaneous, yet disciplined, aspect of creativity, with these areas being equally under the guidance of perceptive senses.

*Wisdom and Integrity vs. Despair and Disdain: Purple and Purple*

In the final course of the chart, the pure purple thread is interwoven through the other colors to show how the vital strengths join forces for the last (possibly twenty-five) years of life. This is all to the good, for graceful aging requires all the strength one can muster. As one old woman who was also a doctor put it, "Growing old is not for sissies."

Even in that all-purple square where wisdom and integrity have been made one's own from the seven earlier stages of the life cycle, there are still those inevitable gray threads to deal with. Much living can bring on intolerance for those who do not share one's own experience and opinions, and disdain has a prideful quality that can prove insolating. A whole lifetime is apparently not sufficient to ensure the openness of true humility. Approaching death can threaten with despair, that sense that passion, vitality, and even time itself are spent—and perhaps ill spent. But we are not without guides here, for the great souls who have lived before us have expressed in poetry, and especially in music, their sense that life's incongruities can be reconciled and bound into a meaningfulness. By tracing the woven threads to the left in the rectangles across the top of the weaving we can indicate what strengths may have accrued during the life cycle that can be mustered to back up flagging wisdom and integrity.

Now we will follow the rectangles of the top row, moving from right to left, observing how the strength colors move into the purple at this last stage of the life cycle.

## Wisdom and Care: Purple and Light Green (Generativity vs. Stagnation)

First, moving horizontally to the left, are the green threads interweaving with the purple—the fruits of the generative aspects of the life cycle, culminating in the years of producing, caring for the next generation, and taking on the responsibilities of the community. Where there are children and grandchildren, the generational sequence is evident and sure. There will, however, surely also be the knowledge of some large or small part in the generating of things, of making and doing, some unique contribution to the maintenance of community and social order that speaks for the fact that your being there made a difference.

But we cannot ignore the reality of the gray threads, which remind us of the lurking sense of stagnation that besets the long generative years. The individual may well feel, for some reason, that he or she was not purposefully enough involved in the productive mainstream of life and remained an inadequate spectator.

## Wisdom and Love: Purple and Red
## (Intimacy vs. Isolation)

We come, then, to the rosy red threads we have used to represent love, intimacy, and passion. They warm the purple as we look back on our lives that have been and still are enriched and encircled by parents, friends, lovers, and children. This is where recollections cluster, the age-old songs of love and loss touch and heal, and tenderness endures. But with aging come inevitably the experiences of the losses of those who are near and caring. A sense of isolation at this late stage can be deep and bitter.

## Wisdom and Fidelity: Purple and Light Blue
## (Identity vs. Role Confusion)

I suspect that if the blue threads in the next square have become too muted with gray, if confusion about one's sense of identity had not somehow been resolved through the long adult years, that might, indeed, be a catastrophe! One can hope that at least a work identity or role may have resolved the issue to some degree. But one is usually also given time in old age to ruminate about the different roles one has unavoidably played and to wisely accept their inevitability. The twenty-five years now offered by scientific progress is a long stretch of time to plan for, and with health and vitality other role possibilities can be appropriate, and even sorely needed. Whistler's mother, with coiffed head and delicate hands neatly folded, is no model for today. It will be more and more imperative for older citizens, of whom there are so many, to take up some of the burdens of the maintenance of the world.

Resiliency is sorely needed here. Perhaps it is the moment still to elect to take the path not previously taken. To accept the role of the stereotypical oldster who demands only care and entertainment is humiliating unless there is real disability.

## Wisdom and Competence: Purple and Yellow
## (Industry vs. Inadequacy)

Assuredly, all the competencies ever mastered play their part in making the last third of life vital, as well as in offering confidence in one's ability to further learn and grow. Competent, vital, healthy elders are going to have to be the shock troops in breaking up the debilitating character of the dependent, needy, "sere and withered" leaves in our society. Certainly the aging person is forced to cope with a relentless disintegration of capacities that forbids some activities. But many appropriate ones remain. Inappropriate is the social role that deprives the individual of the competencies—physical, mental, and social— which he still commands, and encourages the acceptance of the deprivation. The ill, the afflicted, of course, need care. The aging need activity and every opportunity to reinforce their doing, making, teaching—their sense of active competence. To deprive them of this is to underscore all the residual feelings of inadequacy and inferiority with which they have been inevitably coping throughout the life cycle.

## Wisdom and Purpose: Purple and Dark Green (Initiative vs. Guilt)

Looking at the next rectangle of interwoven dark green and purple, one longs for slim threads of real gold that would be intertwined with the green and rise up from the fringed warp at the bottom of the weaving, sparkling all the way up. It would have been appropriate so to have highlighted the lively motivators of this third stage: play, imagination, curiosity, and invention, combined with some previous sense of will, purpose, and trustfulness—these are the components that support continued vital growth in the aging.

If Susanne Langer nominated imagination for the "oldest mental trait that is typically human, older than discursive reason," then I would submit that it must also be the source of that other purely human attribute, namely, humor, that liberating recognition of the absurdities of life. And if on those stages of life one extra player were allowed, not carrying any of the main roles, but ever present, it would surely be the jester with his ironic bells and irrepressible wit. There is healing in laughter, for it expresses our humanity and our wholeness and alerts us against both pride and despair by keeping us in touch with the ridiculous. Old age is a good time for laughter.

However, where overenthusiasm and carelessness of the feelings, rights, or property of others have led to situations involving guilt, this burden may hang heavily in the ruminations of elders. Some great injustice suffered may also persist as a gray memory. Old age is also a good time to talk, to write, to express in any creative medium, and somehow to deal with lingering hurts and irresponsibilities.

### *Wisdom and Will: Purple and Orange (Autonomy vs. Shame and Doubt)*

Now we are returning again to the vital strengths of will and autonomy—those bright orange threads crisscrossing the dominant purple. This was initially the stage when our musculature began to take willful control of our bodies and our space, only to met up with the restriction of concerned, caretaking adults. It was at this time that we had to learn from our kinesthetic sensibility just what we really could master, and we learned this the hard way by trying, failing, and feeling ashamed.

The struggle for mastery is repeated in the years of aging. Perhaps the greatest mistake is to abandon the attempt for fear of shaming. But there must also be realistic assessment of capacities and a sensible relinquishing of some activities for those that are more appropriate. This is indeed a fine time to renew those earlier relationships with materials and things, those art experiences that revitalize all the senses for the services they can still perform and the joy they can give.

### *Wisdom and Hope: Purple and Dark Blue (Basic Trust vs. Basic Mistrust)—The Last Confrontation*

Now to that last left-hand rectangle in this upper row where the dark blue of hope and trustfulness and gray of mistrust and protest weave together with the purple of final maturity. Perhaps there should be a ninth stage indicated, because there is, inevitably, one further challenge. The struggle may be a long or short one, but one would will surely to face it and live it through with integrity. Rainer Maria Rilke's version of this wish is:

> O Lord, give to each his own death,
> That dying which emerges out of the very living
> In which he knew love, sense and want.*

And every devotee of creativity would long to add: and has transcended some of this knowing with a legacy of truth and beauty. Probably Rilke, artist that he was, took that for granted.

No one, of course, has lived to the purple and not inevitably been nudged by the knowledge of this constant dark companion: In the midst of life, however, long-range plans are purposeful and sensible. Later they become peppered with question marks and cautiously signed "S.P."— "Statistics Permitting." If on the long road love, significant work, and laughter have been your lot, along with the anguish and the losses, you can only be grateful. But in that first meeting of "eye to eye" the faith and trust engendered had, of course, an earlier generational source. From generation to generation that "I-to-I" encounter has proceeded from some engendering Source. To return eventually to an Ultimate Source can be a sustaining hope.

One of the great difficulties in translating the poet Rilke is his consistent, purposeful use of the simplest words to express the deepest truths. In the poem quoted above, he uses the words "love, sense and want" (Liebe, Sin und Not). How encompassing and deeply meaningful are these words that sum up for him the significance of life!

We have based the hope-filled development of the life-cycle stages on the receptive love with which the infant is welcomed into this world and on the trust and hope

*Rainer Maria Rilke, *The Book of Hours*. Leipzig: Insel Verlag, 1905.

which this caring nourishes in the newcomer. Gradually, this cornerstone supports an openness to receiving and giving, a mutuality of loving trustfulness. Such mutuality, in turn, engenders a sensible self-love, a pleasurable satisfaction in the developing muscles and senses and the constant stimulation offered by their activation. Without this self-feeling, self-knowledge, there could be little of that empathy which evokes friendship, intimacy, and, finally, caring for and about others. The ancients used two words for our word *love: caritas,* which is charity, an active, explicit caring for; and *agape,* which is a more universal caring about. I believe this latter to be more accurately defined by our word *empathy,* the capacity to feel oneself in the place of another and sensitively to share the urgencies of this other's life experiences. This is not an intellectual achievement, but rather a delving into one's life's storehouse of sense memories and feelings, of awarenesses and perceptivities.

We have spoken at length about the senses and the need for their refinement so that they may provide reliable information to guide intelligent purposefulness. Good sense, we have said, is mandatory for survival, and certainly for all generative endeavors.

Loving and the savoring of relationships, as well as the abundant delights and gifts of the senses, might, however, lead to a kind of inertia of satiation, a kind of Lotus Land. But our senses not only enrich and nourish us, they also signal our needs, which are consistently time oriented and pressing. Each sense makes its own demands, and our bodies are never totally at rest.

And we are not islands. We need others and need to feel needed. We long to be productive and to feel that through our own competent activity we can shape or at least modify our environment. All of us know the need to express inexpressible feelings which well up as we meet life's challenges: the challenges of loss and misadventure which limit and force change and transcendence upon us.

Rilke's words are, then, heavy words, indeed—perhaps the heavier for being so small!

I have translated Rilke's *Not* as *want*, a deeply sensed yearning that is ever present in moments of reflection. Is it a longing to have a part in the world's creative process—to extend oneself creatively into the ongoing, whole-making, healing processes of life? I believe this is what Walt Whitman must have meant when he wrote:

The unknown want—the destiny of me.*

Perhaps it is the quiet function of all art to evoke this stretching, insatiable "want" that is expressed in the creed "I believe in the fulfillment of the sacramental promise that is present in all beauty" (Roger Fry).

I think over again my small adventures.

My fears,
Those small ones that seemed so big.

Of all the vital things
I had to get and to reach.
And yet there is only one great thing,
The only thing:

To live to see the great day that dawns
And the light that fills the world.

—OLD INUIT SONG

*Walt Whitman, "Out of the Cradle Endlessly Rocking," in *Leaves of Grass*.

# 4

# In Defense of
# the Dystonic

> . . . life can be compared to a piece of
> embroidery, of which, during the first half of
> his time, a man gets a sight of the right side,
> and during the second half, of the wrong. The
> wrong side is not so pretty as the right, but it
> is more instructive; it shows the way in which
> the threads have been worked together.
>
> —ARTHUR SCHOPENHAUER*

Regardless of a consistent effort to mention, even to
applaud, the dystonic element present in conjunction with the syntonic basic strength at every stage of the
life cycle, a certain positive thrust seems to prevail. Is it
because we first called these strengths *virtues*, a word we
used because it denoted vitality? Or is an American opti-
mism apparent here—a pervasive accent on the positive
that goes along with the consistent smile for which we
are famous? When any brief review of the eight stages is
discussed, almost invariably only the syntonic strengths
are addressed, and all too often they are presented as
goals or achievements. That the syntonic without the
dystonic is meaningless, and that none of the basic
strengths is ever permanently achieved—these immuta-

* *Counsels and Maxims.* London: Swan Sonnenshein & Co., 1890.

ble truths somehow are never quite understood or accepted. The properties of the dystonic elements not only as they show themselves each at their own critical stage of development, but throughout the life cycle, should be understood and respected.

We have consistently used the word *versus* to suggest the juxtaposition of the syntonic and dystonic elements needing resolution: dependent upon one another yet remaining distant, and with extending distance becoming increasingly incompatible.

William Blake has called these polar opposites *contraries*, whereas modern physics has coined for such polarities the word *complementarities*. These elements pull away from one another, causing tension; yet neither is strong or independent without the counter pull of the other.

In the simple diagrams now introducing each dystonic element, small arrows are intended to represent the push and pull of the constant tension between the two poles. The arrows pointing to a possible extension of the line are important. They suggest that in either direction, if the counter pull fails, the overextension of the line may lead toward an exaggeration amounting to pathology. We will not describe in any detail these malignant or maladaptive possibilities, but only mention them as potentials beyond the dystonic and syntonic. Our purpose has been to clarify how creative energy is generated during the course of normal growth in the tension between the two polarities, which develops into a critical confrontation at each of the eight psychosocial stages of the life cycle.

## In Defense of the Dystonic

| Maladaptive | | Strength | | Malignant Tendency |
|---|---|---|---|---|
| (Sensory Maladaption) ←←← | Basic Trust | Hope | Basic Mistrust →→→ | (Withdrawal) |

vs.

The infant, we have said, is born with instinctual mistrust: appropriate mistrust. There are obvious interior discomforts, as the digestive system and breathing apparatus begin to function. Trustworthy, for the newborn, initially, are all those environmental arrangements which provide the sensation of being back in that warm bath in the former womb matrix.

That early quivering cry to which mothers, particularly, respond so urgently is the expression of the infant's discomfort and need. The mistrust which the cry expresses at this early stage is in the service of survival, and the protest is an inborn survival skill. Infant mortality figures have through the ages been notably high, for vitality and strong lungs are necessary equipment and responsive adults are also mandatory.

But what happens to the infant whose cry is disregarded and whose care is inadequate? When the matrix is too negative, when there is no response to signals of need, no mutuality of contact with caring persons, the infant will withdraw, fail, and die. While some modicum of trust in the environment is maintained, the child will survive but possibly retain a tendency to mistrust unrealistically, which can only be offset by positive experiences later in the life cycle and the support of other developing strengths. As stated repeatedly, every living person survives only if some sense of trust persists and with it, therefore, a promising spark of hope.

But should we weather infancy, how then does mistrust steady our course and maintain our balance? Our powers of perception, which demand the concentrated

1 1 5

attention of every sense for our assessment of people, are all too often slack and careless. We lose the infant's innate, sensory capacity to appraise individuals, which is amazingly acute, and are erringly persuaded by the more superficial appearances and manners. Casual, misplaced trust can be so defeating as to lead to generalized sweeping mistrust. Accurate perception must be cultivated—every sense alert, unimpaired by misuse or stimulant—if it is to serve us in our clear assessment of our own capacities, those of other human beings, and of all the materials and things in our environment. Every drunken driver, one may note, is enormously confident that his are the most acute senses on the road.

Mistrust is our ally, our counterbalance, and a judicious respect for it needs to be maintained as we live with ourselves, our neighbors, and the animal, vegetable, and mineral world around us.

| *Maladaptive* | | *Strength* | | *Malignant Tendency* |
|---|---|---|---|---|
| (Shameless | | | Shame and | |
| Willfulness) ←←←Autonomy | Will | Doubt | →→→ (Compulsion) |
| | | vs. | | |

I suppose that infancy is that short period of human life when we may, with luck, live in Eden, without doubt or shame. With the first great offense, Adam and Eve "hid themselves and were ashamed." So shame came early in the history of humankind, and it comes early in each child's life. Adults, of course, promote this all too carelessly. They are not apt to say to their toddler "Try to feel sorry for Jim because you hurt him with your truck," but "Be ashamed of yourself for what you did." Probably, Adam and Eve said such things to Cain, making him feel

*from God*
*embarrassed*
*or disease*

belittled and "no good"—and that didn't end too well
way back then. Shame seems to surround petty incidents
all through our lives. We blush over trivialities that could
only have loomed large when we were very small and
were made to feel even smaller.

Granted that we begin with this much too early, that
we're quite unrealistic about our expectations of toddlers
and short tempered and unreasonable and all that, but
isn't there a legitimate place for shame? It seems reasonable to postulate that shame began (and still begins) when
man first stood up—the only animal on two feet with free
hands to make things and a head that could remember,
plan ahead, and calculate. But this creature of all creatures was naked and completely exposed. Most animals
have a protective covering, and by walking on four feet
keep out of view, and guard, both genitals and breasts.

*I don't*
*believe this*

Early men began killing animals for their warm hides
and beautiful plumage, and their competitive pride in
those decorated, upright bodies was and still is immense.
Arrogant we are, but not unaware of our dependence on
these borrowed or stolen false feathers which we acquire
only at the expense of others. This awareness shames us
and serves to generate the necessary humility to keep us
human. So shame has its place—a constructive role, if
used in conjunction with pride. "Be too proud to stoop so
low" is a time-honored adage.

And what of doubt? At two, to doubt in one's own fast-
developing physical prowess is judicious. Later, it is still
wise, and in old age absolutely mandatory. Again I would
stress the reliability of sensory experiences as superior to
compliance with the adult's verbal injunction. There must
be leeway for experimentation, for only so do children
really learn. At some point they will surely test out the
veracity of injunctions if not consistently encouraged to
rely on their own sense of experience.

Children should doubt themselves, and they must do this realistically. To have one's capacities doubted by others, especially adults, however, is belittling—can even be stunting—and might challenge individuals of any age beyond the safe limits of their own recognized mastery.

But what is the possible outcome if there were too little curbing of willfulness? Many of us know families where, in the interest of furthering maximum freedom of development, the child is allowed "to rule the roost." This child is being ill prepared for life in a community where interdependence and sharing are mandatory. Neither grownups nor children will want to be with such a domineering person either as a child or later as an adult. Moreover, if the behavior persists the law will step in and exercise its necessary curbs. This is obviously a maladaptive direction to pursue.

However, should shame and doubt, in time, become too pronounced, a malignant consequence could be a sense of compulsion which seriously inhibits freedom and spontaneity.

| *Maladaptive* | | *Strength* | *Malignant Tendency* |
|---|---|---|---|
| (Ruthlessness) ←←← | Initiative | Purpose | Guilt →→→ (Inhibition) |
| | vs. | | |

Guilt and sin, I suspect, are very close. Sin is the old biblical word for the forbidden act performed; guilt is the resulting sense of taint which lives on in the performer. We are ashamed of some exposure of weakness, of being caught in some self-belittling act—and it can be, and often is, a very trivial one. Guilt, however, seems usually to involve someone else's person or right. It is evoked by an act of irresponsibility, malice, or envy.

1 1 8

## In Defense of the Dystonic

When we consider that wonderful third stage of the life cycle pervaded with play, inventiveness, imagination, and creativity—all those vital elements which should be fostered—it is difficult to evoke the concept of guilt. Yet, we well know that these impulses in all their fresh enthusiasm must be bridled, must acknowledge control. Social limits are mandatory; we do not live alone. But all these exuberant manifestations can only be creatively productive if they learn to bow to the universal demands, the authority of form and community.

Purposefulness, too, is acclaimed in old and young. It is one of the major indexes of vital living. But when it becomes ruthless the law moves in and society frowns accusingly. When strictures are too harsh and relentlessly enforced, however, inhibition may result. A fine balance is required on the part of the parents and educators in these matters.

In this technological age we are beginning to shudder at the impetus we have given to innovation. A visit to the moon seems almost playful as we now contemplate what destructive potentials our ingenious scientists have, with our encouragement, created to hang over our future like a veritable bomb of Damocles.

| *Maladaptive* | *Strength* | *Malignant Tendency* |
|---|---|---|
| (Narrow Virtuosity) ←←← Industry | Competence | Inadequacy →→→ (Inertia) |
| | vs. | |

In our competitive society it seems unnecessary to stress the importance of competence. All societies adopt some form of training so that the young may become supporting members of the tribe, community, and the polis. In our Western world we stress literacy, cognitive skills, and the measurable aspects of scientific enterprise. This emphasis, however, fails to promote the discovery and support of the potential of those whose capacities are sharp when involved with inventive imagination and artistic creativity. In either case, industriousness and discipline are mandatory for learning and growth, but such concentration only follows vital involvement.

Where industriousness is focused too early within a narrow frame of study, other possible interests may be closed off, allowing little resiliency for change and promoting a narrow virtuosity. When the schools present a curriculum based on a regimentation of facts which dominates all learning, the danger is that many children with creative capacities and little interest in such a program will be made to feel inadequate and inferior. A sense of inferiority is, however, closely related to humility, which is a necessary approach to learning. However, to be a stimulus, this must be based on a realistic appraisal of personal capacities and a recognition of excellence in others.

When a student is unable to focus involvement and industriousness on any activity or area of study, or when teachers, family, and companions consistently belittle capacities, the resulting sense of inadequacy may elicit a malignant tendency to inertia and disengagement.

Competence does remain a survival strength of major importance.

## In Defense of the Dystonic

| Maladaptive | Strength | Malignant Tendency |
|---|---|---|
| | Role | |
| (Fanaticism) ←←←Identity Fidelity Confusion→→→ (Repudiation) | | |
| vs. | | |

Is it not so that our lifelong struggle to deal with mistrust, shame, and guilt is, though not always hidden from others, still a largely unconscious, interior one? Inadequacy and role confusion, though no less deeply experienced, we share willy-nilly with our families, friends, and companions. We can discuss these encounters between the syntonic and dystonic elements with others at least on a superficial level.

When young people in high school know exactly what way they plan to pursue, that often seems as disappointing as it is encouraging. For some extraneous reason this course may be mandatory—somehow given and clear. This decisiveness promises commitment and an energy and focus which carries an individual a long way. But what of all the doors which had to be firmly closed to make possible this firm commitment? Identity confusion—role uncertainty—although vastly more uncomfortable, suggests a willingness to entertain many roles, many directions, before a more final choice.

I believe that this openness, this flexibility, should remain throughout life. No stage is just what one believed it was going to be. There should be room for the adventure that offers itself. An identity cohesion that sets one in a narrow groove, however successful, may also constrict or even imprison.

A fidelity to a deep inner "I"-ness can remain constant and continuous regardless of the roles that the social matrix imposes. Regular bouts with *a bit* of role confusion may well be salutary.

The maladaptive danger of a too early and firm identity cohesion lies in the possibility of a tendency toward fanaticism. Totalitarian systems demand an all-or-nothing advocacy to which young idealists are prone. If, however, role confusion persists too long, the malignant possibility is that the young, perhaps too protean individual may come to a repudiation of all social roles and remain a consistent and misanthropic adjuster to circumstance.

| *Maladaptive* | *Strength* | *Malignant Tendency* |
|---|---|---|
| (Promiscuity) ←←← Intimacy | Love | Isolation →→→ (Exclusivity) |

vs.

Love, intimacy, and work, it is said, provide life with its essential meaning, without which the world would be a wasteland. But these gifts also make great demands, such as fidelity and responsibility, thus curbing independence and spontaneity. And yet there have been and are great souls who have sometimes braved isolation for the promotion of a course, for religious reasons, or for some more personal reason, to prove to themselves their self-sufficiency. As a chosen path this can be productive and fulfilling. However, most isolates are not necessarily so by choice.

Let us consider, though, what transpires when intimacy becomes too cloying. Two trees growing in close proximity may both be equally malformed or one may quite dominate the space. Growing things need space, and the life-cycle pattern is a growth pattern. Although bleak isolation is an extreme that cannot be generally recommended since it can lead to a tendency toward malignant exclusivity, nevertheless some distance in space, some isolation in time, may be a requisite for balanced living, and certainly for creativity.

## In Defense of the Dystonic

A possible maladaptive tendency, on the other hand, may be an empty and insatiable promiscuity where the deep need for intimacy becomes overwhelming and remains forever unsatisfied.

For the artist, as well as for all other creative persons, there is another aspect of isolation which should be realistically appraised, namely, the failure to reach an audience. Art is intended to communicate—it breathes a message. When this communication seems utterly to fail, two courses are possible. The first may be to maintain one's course and to affirm coolly that the world is not ready for one's work, and this may be right. The second possibility is to ask, "Is my message, the truth I want to convey, stated in such a universal way that others can receive it with empathy?" In either case, a sense of isolation can temporarily block the working impetus of the artist. A pause, then, a drawing back to ask whether one's language is inadequate, too foreign, or too skillful, may be appropriate—or, on the other hand, a decision to brave it out alone with little feedback until . . .

The literature available concerning the lives of artists, creators great and small, may offer a sense of companionship during the dilemma of decision making. The isolation which invades us all now and then can, like the other dystonic pulls, offer a wholesome challenge.

| Maladaptive | | Strength | | Malignant Tendency |
|---|---|---|---|---|
| (Overextension) ←←← | Generativity | Care | Stagnation →→→ | (Rejectivity) |
| | | vs. | | |

The word *stagnation* carries with it such a repugnant odor that one is tempted to settle for *uninvolvement.* However, the sense of stagnation that everyone must experience now and then is truly miserable and utterly depressing—and yet, I would contend, it serves a purpose.

The long span of generativity is steadily challenging in its demands and responsibilities. It really does encompass "the maintenance of the world." Adults must care for the young, their own work, all the social institutions, and the aging—an enormous burden. Vital involvement in all of these facets of life requires stamina.

To withdraw, to repudiate some of these commitments, almost with a sense of self-preservation, is at times a great temptation. This is a signal for reevaluation, for setting up priorities which must include the discipline of maintaining one's own physical well-being.

Care and generativity call inescapably for constant giving and sharing. This can be, of course, rewarding and sustaining when your cup is full and running over. But there are those moments, and sometimes longer periods, when—who can deny it—a drought sets in, and a sense of utter emptiness takes over.

Every artist has experienced this, sometimes immediately following a creative effort full of tension. Then a fallow time of refueling seems to become mandatory—some uninvolvement and reconnoitering in the service of self-recreation.

Overextension, which is the possible maladaptive tendency, can, in the end, be defeating. Tension exhausts, vitality must be forced with stimulants, and true involvement and creativity suffer as well as health.

A sense of stagnation that is more than a respite tends to approach a malignant rejectivity of all societal interactions and associations. This can only be defeating because essentially human beings are gregarious and interdependent and never really self-sufficient.

## In Defense of the Dystonic

| Maladaptive | | Strength | Malignant Tendency |
|---|---|---|---|
| (Presumption) ←←←Integrity | | Wisdom | Despair →→→(Disdain) |
| | | vs. | |

Our first basic strength, you may remember, was hope, the Latin source being the verb *sperare*, to hope. How appropriate, then, to find our form of this word *desperare* as the final dystonic element with which the aging individual must cope. Desperation and hopelessness have usually been the accepted lot of the "sere and withered leaf." How then shall we command the kind of tensile strength which physical disintegration and loss contribute to the last years of life?

One must be a firm believer indeed in what we call progress to see only good in it. When a person has grown old enough—say eighty or so years—so much change has taken place in that life span that it is overwhelming. Don't go back to a city you loved fifty years ago. It is now a ferment of traffic and light and noise, and it is not safe to walk there in the streets alone at night. Even the lovely cities of Europe, preserved like museums for the tourist trade, are tangled with cars and dank with smog, and beautiful Venice sinks back into the sea. Yes, there was something in those "good old days" besides the youthful vitality and the visions of a bright future about which to be nostalgic. Well, a clever, creative new generation will solve these problems, plus water pollution, air pollution, world hunger, and nuclear weapons. So be it!

Should an elder of the tribe feel no despair? We can get to outer space, but we cannot yet feed the children of our own land, much less those who starve beyond our borders.

Have you visited the colonies of senior citizens who

1 2 5

have dedicated their lives to recreation and have withdrawn from the "maintenance of the world" when there is still so much that they could contribute? I am not convinced by those bright smiles and bland faces. Your life cycle is, after all, your most personal creative effort; shouldn't it in some way continue to communicate with all the old and young with whom you have shared this life?

It would indeed be a failure of reality orientation not to be cognizant of our human inability to live together in peace without injustice and violence—not to recognize the enormity of the problems we, the old, are leaving to the coming generations. It is a mortifying legacy. Added to this awareness is the intimate daily hurdle of gathering enough strength to buck physical disintegration, the loss of dearly held friends and places, and all the other challenges of that final, purple stage of the life cycle. Summed up this does present a heavy load. However, in all organic life we witness a struggle to survive, to celebrate life to the last moment. I believe this to be natural wisdom. Despair in some quantity seems inevitable; disdain for what is and has been—no.

However, old age is never a guarantee of wisdom, and those elders who act on such a claim only suffer from a lack of humility which surfaces as presumption.

But I would like to conclude my defense of the dystonic with a further observation. If one were to mesh all the creative strengths to form a personage of great excellence, the result would probably prove quite formidable. I am reminded of the child's prayer: "Please, dear God, help us to be good—and make the good people nice." I would suggest that "nice" for a child and for most of us is a euphemism for describing a person who has strained with persistence to maintain a balanced center and ultimately knows the forces with which one must contend in order to do so. There should surely be some outward and visible signs—traces of the tensions which four score years of living leave on the body, as well as quantities of available empathy for surrounding strugglers. A liberal seasoning with humility is obviously required to make and keep human beings human.

# The Life Stages and
# the Creative Process

All artists know that in the process of working with their
materials, certain problems of unknown origin arise
and block the flow of their work. Feelings of inadequacy
or doubt, sometimes a real wall of resistance, make pro-
ceeding almost impossible. These do not necessarily stem
from the processes themselves, which are often difficult
enough, but from some source undefined and frustrat-
ingly recurring. All artists, I believe, suffer such moments
and periods. I would like to propose that these blocks are
rooted in the essential life-cycle tensions for which the
creative person continues to seek resolutions and this, in
fact, in such a way that they are evoked and can be transcended in the self, in the work, and in a possible audience.

Without further dwelling on definitions, let me offer
an example of the kind of dilemma any artist may have

daily or at intervals. Since we have already dealt with the challenges of process and form, and our relationships with things and materials, we now turn our attention to the personal problems, insecurities which, for example, any author must repeatedly face.

Suppose that the project in hand is a book. The writer has, we presume, been involved with the subject matter for some time and has a great desire, a real yearning to express some ideas in such a way that they communicate with others who share this experience.

How to begin? Some authors begin with the introduction and say clearly what the book is all about and why it was written. These same authors presumably make careful outlines of each chapter and then follow through. Others more intimately known to me write an introduction when the book is finished and they can see what they have written. Chapters are outlined also after the fact, often after they have been reoriented and re-formed several times. This is of course risky, and probably not to be recommended. The method selected is a matter of personality or technique and can be included in what may be called the first flush of inspiration. The real work, in either case, is still to come.

Probably the most unnerving and repeated query to be faced by the author will be, "What made me think this is really such a good and new idea? It will take years to finish such a work, and have I really the stamina to undertake it?" And of course there is the very practical question, "Has this book already been written by someone else?"

Perhaps after looking through publishers' listings and talking to respected advisers the decision is made—"Yes, this is really an original and exciting idea and well worth the doing"—and there follows a great sense of *hope* and vitality. Is this the end of the problem? Oh, no! Every day

1 2 9

as the hand grasps the pen, and especially when the well of words seems to have gone dry, back come those nagging, *mistrusting* questions. These are the mistrusting dystonic questions which will reappear constantly to grapple with the affirming *trust* and *hope*.

To the rescue may come the vitalizing, supportive determination of the second stage, the *willpower* to proceed. Some *doubt* and anxiety will certainly be lurking around at this point: "Do I really know enough to try to do this? Will I be shamed by some of those devastating book reviews?"

At this point a sparkling new thought connection may surface to cheer you, followed by a surge of adrenaline. *Initiative* with its co-instigators imagination, invention, and humor revive you until the notion plagues you, "Has someone already said that? Am I overreaching myself? Is this hubris?" Then ever-ready *guilt* constrains and monitors the free flow of ideas.

"Whatever made me think I could write?" may mark the next all-but-insurmountable hurdle. "I'll never be able to pull this off, I just haven't the skill, the necessary *competence*. Anyway, this pen is miserable and the typewriter old and shabby." But with luck, a reviewing of any past literary success, however minimal, may serve temporarily to muster the courage to proceed in spite of nagging feelings of inferiority and *inadequacy*.

However, here it is important to respectfully defend and even applaud the dystonic elements of these tensions which promote vital strength and growth. The dystonic, I would maintain, actually mobilizes development, and this will be further elaborated later. That much of this juxtaposition of the relationship between the syntonic and dystonic is an unconscious process must also be emphasized. The strengths as they increase with each resolution, however temporary, reliably make further steps in

*good paragraph* [margin annotation]

the creative process possible. This should be trusted. For each individual the critical moments will be found where probably earlier-stage tensions were least satisfactorily resolved. But although the creative process is a stream with many shoals, all obstacles sometimes give way when an impetus of new insight and coherence pushes the flow forward vigorously. Flexibility and playfulness can rise above plodding, stepwise momentum if the project maintains its wholeness and direction.

As the book progresses, the unfortunate writer will nevertheless face not only the tug-of-war between these four early polarities but all the other confrontations spelled out in that psychosocial developmental chart with which we introduced the life cycle. All those childhood struggles must be faced again in a form more or less appropriate to the artist's present age and to the task involved. It is humbling to find that, in facing the writing of that manuscript or book, one is still cringingly apprehensive about failure and dubious about the wisdom of being exposed. And there is a certain guilt about the justification for spending so much valuable time with no certainty as to what will come of it—wondering if the inspired idea will inspire anyone else and whether it has any merit whatsoever. No artist ever feels entirely competent to give form to his or her vision. Perhaps the greatest challenge is the knowledge that the final work *must* be an authentic expression of what one set out to communicate or it will be invalid. It must offer a kind of distillation of the stored sensory and experiential knowledge which has been stashed away and waiting for this moment since childhood. For only from that material can one create with authority and integrity.

The word validity leads us into the fifth stage, that bridge between childhood and adulthood where the strength to be fostered is *fidelity* and the opposite pulls to deal with are *identity* versus *role confusion*. Here the uniqueness of each individual takes form and grounds each eventual identity firmly in loyalty to ideals, convictions, and possible goals. A shifting confusion weakens any hope of developing a personal "way" or social direction.

For the artist this poses a major hurdle since to create anything that does not generate from what is uniquely one's own is not genuine. Integrity demands that what is produced is based on experience validated by trustworthy senses. The struggle to maintain this fidelity is awesome since our schooling has neither emphasized nor promoted such confrontation. Facts are presented and learned and at best one can hope to quote the current "authority." Without experiential knowledge one is on very shaky ground, which is the construction business is called "fill" and risky.

The confrontation of *intimacy* and *isolation* in the sixth stage reaches for the artist into his or her personal life. Since feelings are highly charged in all creative activities, intimacies inevitably set a tone for the work in hand. However, there is a special intimacy between the artist and the medium which is used to express the vision or idea to be developed. This relationship can grow into a genuine *love*. Writers love words, potters clay, sculptors stone and wood. I don't believe that this is a mere form of speech. But when there are stagnant periods the intimacy seems temporarily lost and a sense of dreary *isolation* besets the would-be artist.

*Generativity* should, beyond anything else, generate the strength of *care*, a caring for and about everything in the matrix of the individual. For the writer-artist this means that, beyond all the responsibilities of the "maintenance of the world," the work itself must be a dominant focus of caring. The writing, revision, criticism, and perhaps publication of each project must be a matter of consistent concern. It is all too easy to grow weary and relax into a short or prolonged state of *stagnation.* Aging does nothing to lighten this problem and temptation. And so we come to *wisdom.* I believe that old artists, and writers of course, have the best that life has to offer in old age because nothing but decrepitude forces them to give up their work. The struggle continues, however, because maintaining *integrity* and integration in spite of disintegration is a major challenge. Too keep hope dominant in spite of the obvious reasonableness of *despair* is nothing short of superhuman. The *love* for the medium is strengthening, the *care* about and for what has been produced is challenging, and *wisdom* demands that you don't give up.

Now are these humiliating struggles an asset or something to deplore? Consider the cool arrogance of the artist who seems to rise above this very normal struggle in which all human beings are involved. Such virtuosity might astound but also bore us thoroughly. Flawlessness in handmade objects arouses some suspicion and little empathy.

It is, of course, a surprising property of humility that it stimulates innovation and learning and permits playfulness. Now, every artist knows that each work is one great moment of play-related inspiration and hours and days at least of hard work. A medieval monk, bearing no responsibility for either the content or the form of the "holy writ" he copied, has left us this testimony of his trials: "Writing is excessive drudgery. It crooks your back, dims your sight, twists your stomach and your sides. Three fingers write, but the whole body labors."* This drudgery, I would submit, involves the struggle for disciplined

*G. G. Coulton, *Social Life in Britain from the Conquest to the Reformation.* Cambridge, England: Cambridge University Press, 1919.

competence, and that is a high priority. But it concerns also the mustering of the stamina needed for facing the constant tension between the contradictory pulls presented by the challenges of the life stages. While growth and constant change continue to tip the scales, these tensions never find more than temporary balance. It is, I believe, this very tension that keeps us seeking and renewing, that spurs becoming and creating, for these syntonic and dystonic elements are vital to one another. They are the north and south poles of our psyches—complementarities which attract, define, and provide the "rigor and unity of the form needed to contain them."

These last words appear in William Gibson's book *Shakespeare's Game,** and he goes on to write: "Is it too much to say that in examining drama as a form we are in the playpen of contradiction itself, that is, willy-nilly are contemplating its nature as a dialectic in the mind?—which cannot be irrelevant to the mystery of the creative gift."

This is indeed an arresting statement! Consider the phrase "playpen of contradiction." How could one express more felicitously when and where the struggle begins and how it must be viewed and appreciated as essential to the creative process as well as to growth itself?

If then, as we have said, the product is a genuine expression of the doer or maker, it will provide for her a relief from the tension between the syntonic and dystonic elements in her which were in explicit disharmony. The most perfect resolution for anyone should be the one appropriate and possible for the age and degree of mature skill of the producer and performer. A five-year-old's painting could be, therefore, a five-year-old's master-

---

*New York: Atheneum, 1978.

piece. A seventy-year-old's masterpiece might, for example, be Rembrandt's portrait of himself at that age.

The creative *process*, when carried through with genuine involvement, including attention, discipline, and complete respect for the laws which govern matter, will inevitably tend to resolve the tension in the psyche of the doer and maker in such a way that further growth is enabled. Each temporary resolution which increases the strength of the "virtue" ready to be developed is a source of stability for the next stage. The balancing of these syntonic and dystonic elements, these forever incompatibles, is what generates the conception and enlivens the resulting art form.

With each successive creative undertaking, the opportunity is provided to revitalize once more the accrued strengths of the life-cycle stages. Thus, we prepare for the next day. Moreover, the great works of art, and many which are less acclaimed, sustain and nourish us all, restoring the trust, hope, and compassion which we lose in the petty dealings of daily involvements. In great works of art we honor simultaneously the struggle of the process undertaken, the stamina and authority of the artist, and the integrity of the vision manifested.

It has seemed necessary to ruminate about all of this within the context of the creative process. However, reinforced with the knowledge of the universality of this experience, we still are no way able to truly comprehend the miracle of creativity. Let us not try to. The deepest truth in the end probably is that we can and must trust it.

## ❧ 6 ❧

# Three Artists Speak

Now, if these detailed descriptions of the problems involved in just growing up haven't exhausted you, you will hear the voices of three professional artists. They are alive and creating and all of them are very close friends. When I urged them to share their thoughts and feelings about this work with all of us I had only vague plans in mind about the contents of this book. As it goes to press they have still not seen the manuscript. I am deeply grateful for their confidence that the setting will not embarrass them in any way.

How shall I introduce these friends I have known for so long? They all live as artists live, which is creatively—taking themselves lightly but nevertheless always very seriously in every detail as far as their creativity is concerned. Social demands are met, but with humor in order not to become conspicuous. Nothing is done in slipshod fashion. Every created thing appears with fingerprints somewhere in the finished project like a personal signature.

Leo Garel's studio is his house. It is in no way sedate and the lucky visitor may feast on finished, near-finished, unmounted, and sometimes framed paintings.

Joan Loveless manages house, weaving room, and a garden. Her head is also full of grandchildren. Sheep she knows about and has shorn. She told me the memorable story about the Indian woman who hurried back to her hogan full of immense laughter and said to her mother, "There was this white woman who bought my blanket and asked if I would sell my loom. And do you know what? She doesn't even have any sheep."

Maia Aprahamian is also Mary Lynn Twombly. The first is her composing name, her musical self. Music is her raison d'etre, but her life includes family and friends and many community involvements. I hear music in her words as if all were set in a form not recorded in notes but audible to the reader.

Sharing these friends with you, my readers, is a great privilege.

# Leo Garel, *Painter*

Looking back over my life the most consistent thread that runs through it all is that I've always been an artist. This has not been at all practical. At times I've felt as though I've had to support this need the way a drug addict has to support his habit.

My earliest memories are of drawing, way before I started school, and later when I was in the first grade I looked up in surprise at the teacher watching me drawing instead of doing my lesson. She made me sit in the wastebasket as a punishment.

The artist is completely out of the whole economy of supply and demand. You continue to paint pictures whether there is a market for them or not. The most successful artists leave hundreds of unsold pictures when they die. Though I've enjoyed the other professions I've been in, I certainly wouldn't be engaged in them unless I was paid. I've never ever thought of using a standard of money in considering continuation of painting.

As a boy drawing was an obsession and I was constantly with a pad and pencil. My father was concerned and kindly suggested that maybe I shouldn't draw all the time since I might get tired of it. "Draw once in a while then rest and draw again in a few days." I ignored his sympathetic advice.

What is the attraction that painting has for me? It'll have to be a partial answer because the artist is always expressing much that is different from his intention and I don't pretend to be fully aware of the mystery of creation. However, I do know that it is one of the areas in which it is possible to be totally your own man, to reject anything, to follow any whim in attempting to discover yourself and yet not hurt anyone through this selfish self-indulgence.

In high school art appreciation class I was outraged and intrigued to hear that the most important criterion of a portrait's worth was not a likeness. I never knew of any other purpose in doing a portrait and it was the only goal I'd been using.

The painting is always a vehicle for a deeper, self-expressive meaning and it is impossible for the artist not to reveal himself. Even a portrait of someone else is also a portrait of the artist. Though the artist thinks he is only concerned with specific outside relationships, like the sitter's length of nose, he paints himself, too. When I say a Rembrandt portrait, a Renoir portrait, a Van Gogh portrait, you know exactly what I mean.

When I went to art school I began to experiment with form. My father said to me: "I went for a walk in the park and watched an artist painting a scene which was exactly like what I saw. Why can't you be an artist like that?" I was dismayed and didn't know what to answer, but my mother spoke up sharply: "Do you know what a shyster lawyer is?" My father answered: "Yes." "Well, Leo doesn't want to be a shyster artist!"

Possibility and necessity. The critic deals in possibilities and measures a painting in terms of all sorts of principles. The artist deals in necessities and must work for results that are true and valid for him, often only by rejecting principles that he's learned.

I wondered whether to paint shapes which were non-objective or forms which were abstracted from appearance or should I use reality with a design substructure? Maybe I should paint thin with a hard edge or maybe I should paint loosely and thickly? Which direction was art going? What was the most logical method? Questions like these kept me from sleeping. Then in the middle of the night I suddenly had a simple revelation: This was not a logical decision for me to make. I must paint only in a way that is natural for me. I had to find out who I am in paint.

There is a paradox which is the essence of our being. All people are exactly alike; each person is unique and special. In painting it is possible to be absolutely personal, to find an original form which is specifically your own and through this new statement stir and communicate with others. Not everybody, but then, nobody does.

After finishing art school I announced to my family that I was going to be a serious artist, not a commercial one. They were upset and anxious for me. My brother-in-law exclaimed: "Are you going to be a bum all your life?"

Taste is a pleasing arrangement of shapes and colors. Works of art are not based on taste, but on tensions, tensions which are the resolution of conflicts.

I used to look at illustrations and advertisements which were extraordinarily well done, which had fine composition, lovely color, beautiful form and rhythms, and yet were obviously not works of art. I admired their craft, but I wondered about their emotional emptiness. Now I know that in good part it is because they are created with exquisite taste, not tensions.

Then there is the paradox of destruction and creation, intertwined with each other, so very close and yet so very far apart. I feel one cannot exist without the other in my painting. I'm always destroying for creative ends. I'm constantly changing the picture, destroying it in order to bring it to a higher and deeper level of creation. But you take the risk of destruction being the end.

My wife walked into the studio and asked, puzzled: "What

happened to the lovely picture I saw on your easel ten minutes ago?" I shrugged my shoulders: "I tried to improve it, one change demanded another, and soon the painting unraveled."

Painting is full of paradoxes. Your style is made up of your limitations and your strengths. You must preserve the flatness of the surface, yet you must deal with the illusion of space. Symmetry and ugliness. Movement and balance. Line and mass. Simplicity and complexity. The color should maintain the quality of the paint, but it should also be atmosphere. Though it is possible to speak of these all as separate elements, in painting they all must be unified into one inseparable force.

When questioned about my method of painting I am reminded of the centipede who couldn't walk when he tried to figure out how he moved his many feet in harmonious unison.

You have hydrogen and oxygen, but you don't have water until they are combined in an exact way and then there is an exciting, new, indispensable element. What combines all the separate and contradictory forces that go into a painting and makes it into an exciting new element? Simple feeling. Our feelings are magically able to compress all the complexities of our experiences into an elegant unity that becomes a direct statement, a painting.

I tried building a house by myself, but got so in debt for the building materials that I had to take a job with the contractor, who sold me the supplies to pay his bills. For a year I worked as a carpenter, not being able to paint. Every day I did what the foreman told me to do. It was hard work, but I never spent such an easy year. Not having to discipline myself, not being concerned with ultimate values, no guilt in wondering whether what I was doing had meaning, no constant search for creative truth. How restful. Very easy? Yes. Fulfilling? No!

There is the opposition of failure and success. There is hardly a painting I work on which doesn't at some time feel like a complete failure. What keeps me going is not the evidence in the picture, but a sense of belief in myself that stubbornly persists until the picture suddenly arrives at a realization. In fact, I don't trust a picture that comes too easily. Yet all signs of the struggle must be integrated into freedom and ease. The picture must look as though it is immediate and flowing. Another paradox united.

Somebody came up to me at one of my exhibitions and said: "What fun you must have!" Fun? All this labor and desperation, fun? Yet as I looked at my paintings I realized that if they didn't seem like fun, they would not be finished.

There are two reactions (among many) that I have at each of my one-man shows and they are simultaneous. I feel: "What a lot of work, I'll never be able to do this again." At the same time I feel: "Is that all there is? I've accomplished nothing!" Every show is followed by a few depressed, doubtful weeks, but then I'm back at work with renewed vigor.

A Finnish woman, who had not been long in the country and still had trouble with our language, asked me: "Are you going to have an exposure this year?" How much more apt a word than exhibition. When I have an exhibition every one of the paintings seem like a butterfly in a collection, pinned against the wall. And every one of those butterflies is me.

To use another chemical allusion: Salt is made up of sodium, a corrosive substance that eats metal, and chloride, a deadly gas. Combined together they make salt, which is so useful and adds so much flavor for all mankind. Painting is like that. It is made up of the sorrows and chaos of people, but transforms them into order and beauty.

My sister died of cancer and I was very sad. I painted a

picture called *My Sister and the Angel of Death*. I looked at this picture recently and was surprised at its lyrical quality.

Though painting means much to me, there are also obligations to your children (that's creation, too) and you must make the money to pay for the necessities of food, shelter, and clothing for them as well as yourself.

Painting by itself never gave me an adequate income so I did some cartooning. I made enough for me, my wife, and first child, but when a second baby was due I was worried that a free-lance living was not enough. I got a steady job teaching art, too. My brother-in-law (another one, this time my wife's relative) said: "Well, Leo is finally settling down, he's taken a regular job—one day a week."

Being an artist is a way of life, a total involvement that is ingrained in your whole existence. Working on a painting in front of an easel is only a small part (though a very important part) of the creative process. You sum up the accumulation of your experiences at that concentrated time. But you are experiencing as an artist when you are not painting.

I was ill with the flu and for a week couldn't do anything at all, just lie in bed. I thought it was a wasted week since I accomplished nothing. During this time I napped during the day, so got up very early, as soon as the sky started to lighten. I experienced the special sunrise of every morning. Not only was the color of the light different each day, but it changed from moment to moment. This was a rich experience and it led to several paintings as soon as I was well and able to work.

A simple form of life like the one-celled amoeba can perform all its functions through this one cell. It has no limbs, but it can move at will; it has no mouth, but it can imbibe food and digest it without a stomach. As life becomes more evolved from the worm to the fish to the reptile, there are ever more complicated groups of cells which make separate organs for these functions. In man there are complex organs for almost all our needs, but there is one important function for which there is no center—that is our emotional life. When we are upset our blood pressure may rise, we may start to sweat, our hair stand on end, our stomach rebel. Like the amoeba, our whole system is used to express this feeling. What I think art may be is man creating an outer organ for his inner feelings. A concrete structure with form and order for what is amorphous within him. A beautiful vessel for his emotional obscurity.

A landscape that I had just seen interested me and I began painting it in my studio (I do a lot of walking, but paint my experiences indoors) at Woodstock, New York, where I was living at that time. As usual, I was changing the picture for deeper expression when subtly a memory of Taos, New Mexico, began to emerge. I hadn't lived there for over twenty years, but it slowly took over the painting. I always let the picture go where it will.

As I grew older it became obvious to me that I had illusions that I must give up. When I was young I was sure that I would shake the world. It was clear that this wasn't happening and it was not the world's fault. It is painful to give up illusions, but it had to be done. My painting has been a distillation toward my real being.

It is much better to be a real live blade of grass than a papier-mâché oak.

The present fashionable psychological talk about the left-brain, right-brain, creative-intellectual concept and the do-it-yourself art books that suggest exercises with either hand to improve your imagination, I think are a joke. I know firsthand (no pun intended) about this because I had a brain tumor operation several years ago that forced me to change from painting with my natural right hand to the holding of my brush with my left hand. It had no effect whatsoever on my creativity.

A society for the handicapped raises money by selling greeting cards painted by people who must hold the brush in their mouths or with their feet. These are ordinary, well-done, academic cards and I would never know there was anything special about the picture until I read the strange, heart-rending descriptions on the backs. Art has nothing to do with physical action; it is a philosophy, an emotional act, a whole view of life summed up in a visual form.

Sometimes I hit a work block and have absolutely no ideas for another painting. I'm sure that I've painted my last picture. I try to console myself by saying: "What will it matter to anybody if you never paint again." But I'm not consoled and it *does* matter to me. These are uncertain and confused periods, though actually they may be very productive times. They may mean I am tired with what I have been doing, but have no vision of my new painting. Somehow, usually with the lavish help of destruction and the use of the accident (the accident is no longer an accident if you preserve it and then it becomes part of your own arsenal), I work out of these blocks and begin to paint freshly again.

A friend once asked me: "Have you ever considered giving up painting?" "Many times." "How come you never have?" "I never found anything so interesting."

However, interest isn't all the nourishment that painting has given me. Much more: emotional release, renewed vitality, freshness, form, cohesion, integrity, dignity. Even the struggle seems meaningful.

# Joan Loveless, *Weaver*

When I am weaving in the morning and the work is going well—images building and tantalizing drifts and hints of the forms to come darting past—my mind races here and there, to other projects, other materials and forms, and I have to pull it back to weaving. My energy is high, the cello music on the radio is soaring and delving, and the shapes I'm working on are beginning shapes and could go anywhere. Also, my mind plucks at this and that string to avoid finalizing the shapes I'm working on too soon, to keep the choices open and let the paths the weaving takes remain free for longer—to find the *other* alternative, the not-yet-seen way.

My mind in its flight sees my lovely granddaughter, Rochelle, and a tapestry for her begins. I see a kind of veiled surface rising, a surface of naturals back and forth horizontally—a lighter, a slightly darker or different tone—and, as though the weaving is a web, I part it here and there and rounded shapes appear in the openings, perhaps clear light blues, the lovely unknown of her life. I must weave it for her soon; I'll start spinning for it—naturals—and dreaming up the blues.

Now I know I've started to weave again. Across my loom are two orange shapes building and between them are three pale to rich golden brown shapes, one turning back to orange by way of a bit of rosy brick color to make the end of the tan less final. As I work, a wonderful thing is happening which I didn't know I was missing. All the areas across the weaving are building at once. I bring one up a few rows and as I glance away to look at one on the far side of the warp I am caught unawares just enough to realize what really should be done next on the one I looked away from and a good new turn for the shape to take occurs to me. And suddenly I realize that this is what has been missing—this interdependence of the parts, this getting involved in the part of the part—building the shapes not as solids *(things)* but as growing events. So I continue working across my warp keyboard, five small balls of yarn lying on the free warp. I had been impatient, wanting to complete a shape, a decision, until I realized that this was precisely what I needed, what had been missing—this flowing back and forth to build the whole and keeping the communication open between the parts—truly open.

Tapestry weaving has the built-in difficulty that one can work on only one level at a time, the weaving progressing across the entire width, from the bottom (usually) to the top. I can weave only so far with a form before I must go back and bring up the rest of the total before going ahead. Since I don't use cartoons, don't usually in any concrete way design ahead, my images are purely "perhaps" images which actually determine the *direction* I go in. My drawings are exercises, almost like playing scales, establishing a visual mood and perhaps sketching a particular *shape problem* that I want to deal with. Often it happens, though, that the shape problem or visual mood that I begin with does not appear till some later tapestry, or it becomes transformed into a variation which becomes more intriguing and with which I work instead.

When I had just begun this tapestry, working in rich close oranges and deep reds, I had put in some bits of lavender and a bit of light blues and at the end of the day my son, Conor, came in when the weaving was dropped down for looking at the day's work. He said, "Wow, I like those blips of color—but don't do too much of them now!'' So that was a good clue that I was on the right track.

I've spun most of the yarn for this tapestry, partly because I seem to have an immense supply of raw wool around the studio. But mostly I'm spinning it to get immersed in it. It's been a long time since I've woven and I need to spin my way into it. First I dyed up a batch of oranges, brewing and mixing skeins in several pots, trying to get many steps of orange—rosy ones, bright light ones, rusty ones, and some browned enough to be close to a few brownish reds I'm going to use. What I'm really after is colors that I can't easily name—strange colors. It's good when I can't predict just how they'll look when they are together, which direction they'll go in. Then they demand real attention and direct their own handling and create surprises for me, leading me where I had not planned to go. This is what I really like— having something happen in the weaving that I didn't expect and having to really study it and figure out how to use it— how to pick up on it if it is intriguing and find the direction it will lead me in.

Problems usually come up. In this, I'm weaving along playing five or six oranges together, absorbed in their small differences and building beginning shapes. Toward the end of the day I'm tired, have used up my eyes, and suddenly realize that I've gotten into the trap of unrelieved orange. All those luminous colors are darkening. I've run out of leavening and take two days off from weaving to spin. I need a slightly colored neutral, maybe a faintly dyed bluish color. I spin directly from the fleece, without carding, so the yarn will take the dye unevenly and the color even more faintly. My spinning wheel faces the loom and I can keep the weaving in view as I spin. It still looks problematical, though a night's sleep has rid my eyes of the overdose of looking at orange.

After I dye a few skeins of faint bluish, I realize that that won't work and put it aside for later. The solution turns out to be a very lightly dyed combination of golden brown and dark brown. I spin more and go back to the loom with two batches of faint warm colors, one with a bit more brown and one a bit more golden. It's always good to use little enough dye; this literally took only a few sprinkles of dye powder. Usually when I'm dyeing I get carried away with the colors and dye some that don't fit into the piece I'm working on and I set them to the side to wait their turn. I like that, as my mind begins to work secretly on them and I gradually add to them as I do up batches of yarn.

When I went back to the tapestry I wasn't at all sure it would work and had prepared myself for cutting the warp, unraveling the weaving, and beginning again. But it did work! The light, slight colors immediately breathed air into the oranges, combining with them for a while and then opening into a totally light area for a while before bringing the oranges in again, gradually. It's been a good working week. I've been able to start working early when my attention is clearest and to work long days, blending spinning, dyeing, and weaving, which helps all three. I work hard to keep the neutrals active. Now that they're in they have to hold their own or they'll slip into background and I don't want that.

One of the things that I have to work hard at is to diminish the discrepancy between the imagined image and the final *produced* image. Often I seen clearly a beautiful form that I wanted to weave—get just a glimpse of it—and then set out to execute it and find my image gone, or not what I thought it to be. I may be that the problem is in not examining the image carefully enough to understand it, in trying to make the jump from a subtle thought to a constructed image too suddenly. Perhaps I leave out steps and therefore lose it. I must learn to gradually nurture it and go through the stages of mentally interpreting it—of *materializing* it—

before subjecting it to the difficulties of being actually reproduced in materials, yarns. In the mind the image had an environment—mood, thoughts that preceded it, even what one was doing when the image presented itself. All these were part of the circumstance of the image and even if it is a workable idea it needs clarifying, isolating, to check whether it is an *idea* or a *reaction*.

Finally the piece is done and it does indeed stand on its own. When a tapestry is successful I can study it and finally realize what has gone on in it. Then it makes its link to the next one. Curiosities are evoked by it which create a next beginning, not necessarily related in color or even in form, but while the process of working with the phenomena of that tapestry is still fresh in my mind I peruse it for those set-aside thoughts that came and went as I worked. And I find suggestions of shapes, of mood, of color when the work is ended and hung on the wall that set me going again.

# Maia Aprahamian, *Composer*

The act of creation is like the act of love. It asks first for commitment, for risk, for a certain amount of abandon and joy, and for an absolute belief in its integrity of being. For me, there is no such thing as a tentative creation. Every piece of music is the one and only at that moment, whether it is a humorous ditty for a whimsical event, a work for children to sing and play, or a full-length opera, demanding perhaps years of involvement.

To look at this process of creation is a difficult thing, somewhat like trying to observe yourself walking; you know where you start from, you know what you see around you en route, and you know when you get there. But what you are actually doing in the walking is not observable. If you tried to observe it, you would stop—a little like the seeming paradox in physics of the inability to observe certain particles without either affecting them or invalidating the data. So one creates out of a certain amount of assumption—you know where you are by what you see around you, rather than what you are actually doing! So if you, as the reader, are willing to accept my "assumptions" on this journey, I will attempt to describe what I see as the process of creation.

"In the beginning was the Word"—in the Greek it is *logos,* a much more profound concept than the verbal implications of *word.* As a composer, the initial idea comes as a burst—the "logos" or completed and fully enfleshed work, minus any of the practicalities of how it will be expressed!

It is a little like the comic strip "I see!"—the aha!, which can be a blinding flash, or just a little pinprick in the dark. If one is really "turned on" to the idea, then one begins to test it out—to put down all of the ideas that come flying in out of the dark, and to test them in the context of the work. Musical themes, harmonic structures, sometimes whole sections come forth, to be used or not used as the work progresses. Sometimes it is so clear that one just begins to write, and doesn't stop until it is finished, often with very few changes. But this is rare indeed, and must be seen as pure gift.

In the actual writing, there is a combination of the known and the unknown. I often see the structure of a work, and then have to fight to not fall into a pattern of conventionality. Then there are the moments of surprise, when an unexpected theme or chord just appears, and you know it is right. For a beginning composer, there is often just relief at getting the notes—any notes—on paper. But after a certain amount of practice, one wrestles with the angel until the right "note" comes forth. It is a curious combination of the known and the unknown, and must be wooed with care, lest the angel should win! The abstraction of an idea, or the grandioseness, or a variety of other overwhelming categories, may cause the composer or creator to lose all control of the process, and this generally leads to a lack of communication of the idea at a level that is comprehensible to others.

At some point, the work does take on its own life, and one has to let go of control to a certain degree, and become partners with it. There is a marvelous freedom in this—one is always so much richer in that sense of exchange and interaction. There is always an appropriateness to the form that a work takes, and one must take care not to try to stuff it into some other preconceived form. When it has reached this point, it takes sheer perseverance sometimes to carry it through. How tempting it is to bask in the potential and the "almost done." But at this point also, and at any other point in the process of creation, there can come a dry place—the proverbial desert where *no* idea is right, and nothing seems to work. I have found it takes a combination of futile struggling, and just walking away from it. One without the other doesn't work, but I have no idea why. It's often tempting to quit, or just put it aside and never get back to it. But eventually "the desert shall blossom as the rose," and one never knows when that rainfall will come.

The materials of music are as much in the colors of the instruments as in the line of the themes and the texture of the harmonies. There is as much power in dissonance as in consonance, and sometimes the use of certain instrumentation with its own peculiar nuances of overtones and textural qualities can produce a dissonant effect which would not be so with a different instrumentation. This is where the drama of music lies for me, and also in the interweaving of themes and the highlighting of harmonies. Rhythmic structure can do the same—what is majestic in a 4/4 time can turn banal in 3/4. And the use of less conventional rhythmic patterns, with little relationship to the human heartbeat or pulse, can create a kind of excitement that is unequaled by any amount of volume. These are the materials that make the language of music such a universal communication system. It is said that in the higher frequencies of sound and color and light, they become indistinguishable—which means, of course, that that potential is also present at *any* frequency. I suspect this is where such terms as "the dance of the universe" and "music of the spheres" have their originating impulse. If so, then music can be seen (and heard) as one of the highest organizing principles of the universe, and also have the potential for the creation (or un-creation) of chaos. In any case, it nears the premise with which I began this discussion—that there is a "logos," an organizing principle, to all creation, and it most probably is present "in the beginning."

I have to close with one last thought in all this, for having both children and songs and symphonies out in the world, I cannot but be struck by the similarity—both of producing them, and letting them go. It is this last thought that has to occur at the end of any work, no matter how much one wants to hold on to it and refine it or control it. A piece of music has to live on its own, as does any work of art, in whatever form. By the same token, we are all the created "works of art" as the children of earth. Yet have you ever known the paint to turn on the canvas, or the instrument to destroy the player, or the composition to poison the composer? The missing element in all of us today is that of respect. To be creators, or to be created, is to have the utmost respect for that which brings forth and is brought forth. And this may in some philosophical way be what lies behind "logos" itself: a respect for the elements of creation, which binds them into a greater expression of that inner organizing principle, however harshly or humanely honed and resurrected out of the materials of existence.

Call it Word, call it logos, call it brainstorm, or call it God; there is a something that preexists for every moment of creation. And if one is a practical composer or artist of any type, you don't question it too deeply! You just get to work—and enjoy it—and are grateful.

# Wisdom

Wisdom is a word we use almost as casually and even glibly as the word *love*, yet serious consideration would place both among the most revered words in our language. The abuses of the word *love* are too many and obvious to spell out here, but we may presume to clarify, to some degree, the various implications of the word *wisdom*, and perhaps by clarifying the one we may also throw some light on the other.

Dictionaries suggest "clever," "knowledgeable," and "learned" as possible synonyms of this word *wisdom*, and colloquially we have "wise guy," "wise acre." However, when philosophers undertake to clarify what "to be a wise woman or man" has meant traditionally and universally, they resort to such phrases as "to have vision," "to say true."

Seeing and speaking, then, communicate wisdom;

seeing the future as well as the past with the perspective of long years, speaking the word that states the truth.

With these rather unspecific guidelines, one may venture a search for the indices of the roots, the vestiges of wisdom which may be apparent at the various stages in the life cycle by virtue of the fact that, as discussed earlier, the senses offer an experiential source of wisdom. However, this only holds true when the senses are accorded a fundamental attention, and their acuity has been fostered, maintained, and accurately assessed.

I have been affirming the sensory, perceptive, and creative ways to increase in wisdom, to become one who has vision and says true—a way that time has confirmed. However, where among the principles of social order does wisdom find its place and play its role?

Every facet of our social order strives to function under its jurisdiction. Its dominance is sought and even proclaimed in our most revered documents of social principles. "We the people (in our corporate wisdom) do declare" begins the statement of our convictions and purpose as a body politic. Every document, international, national, state, or civic, if it has a preamble, begins with an appeal to or an assertion of wisdom. We claim wisdom as an attribute that permeates our approach to the related institutions of social order and in word, if not always in deed, we find it there.


## Ancient Sources

With all this acclaim and even reverence, where should the seeker after truth look for a cultural repository of wisdom, to find information or affirmation recorded and in some way manifested?

Throughout time and everywhere on the globe, people

have earnestly and with great labor undertaken to pass on, to store, to preserve their nuggets of truth, of wisdom. They remain embedded in myth, legend, song, and poetry, carved in hieroglyphs and in cave paintings. In some written form they have been enshrined as "sacred writ" and "relic" housed in such edifices as tombs, temples, mosques, monasteries, cathedrals, and churches—themselves all endeavoring to manifest their own aesthetic truth. We can find documentation of these records in our great libraries and now in smaller ones, too, as all verbal knowledge becomes translated and disseminated. Computers and microfilm also increase our capacities to store and make available great riches previously unavailable.

Yet how does the wisdom of the serenely quiet, enlightened old ones seep into the social fabric? Does the enduring wisdom of the ages somehow seep down into the groundwater where vigorous roots can seek and find nourishment? I have claimed that the cooperation of the senses in the doing and making of art activities establishes the fabric which holds together the individual (like threads in a weaving). Possibly this even spreads into the social realm so that the creative process and the arts play their roles in holding together the larger social fabric itself. Or does the life cycle act as a quiet transmitter of values that are never put into word or form, but suddenly emerge in serene old men and women?

Something like this, it seems, must be going on, for society has otherwise no outward and visible means of tapping this accrued wisdom of its elders, who have left behind neither written words nor cherished artifacts.

The arts are honored and acclaimed as a universal, perhaps the only universal language, each true form representing the highest and deepest expression of one of the senses in cooperation with the others.

A deep need appears to exist in humankind to grasp

and give auditory, visual, kinesthetic, and plastic form to sensations and ideas that unless grounded in the senses and stored in long-term memory become evanescent; an expression, no doubt, of our constant struggle to deal with loss and change. Memory fades and the need is urgent to communicate with, be recognized by, and record for posterity—to make permanent these deeply sensed experiences.

Aesthetic creations are described in terms of authenticity, strength, uniqueness, wholeness, integrity; and when their colors, spatial configurations, and shadings are felicitously interrelated, we experience "beauty." Years ago John Keats summed up his creed memorably: " 'Beauty is truth, truth is beauty,'—That is all ye know on earth, and all ye need to know." Since all human beings have sought beauty even as they have valued and searched for truth, they must indeed together be subsumed in one quest.

Surely there is a "saying true" in all "true" art that speaks to us individually and collectively of the wisdom of the ages in a language that is comprehensible to all, increasing our sense of the wholeness and continuity of life.

We have no way of knowing whether the great religious figures and philosophers of antiquity were old men and women—old in our terms. We read that Lao-tze wandered off by himself as an old man leaving behind forever the society he knew. However, a few hundred years ago, fifty years was considered to be "ripe old age." Now we consider people to be at the height of their powers in adulthood well beyond fifty. Many of our greatest artists have maintained their vital involvement in their art well into later years without the work losing its unique caliber. We have, in this century, witnessed the enduring productivity of Arturo Toscanini, Georgia O'Keeffe,

*what's yar point?*
*Do you have to be old to be wise?*

Martha Graham, and Pablo Picasso. Homer and Dante, who seem almost mythical, we think of as ancient men of great vision. Perhaps we should ascribe to outstanding not-yet-old figures and artists such as Mozart and Blake the precocious wisdom of "one wise beyond his years," and at the same time admit that becoming old in no way guarantees true wisdom or even some semblance of most of the attributes we may ascribe to it.

## Archetypal Figures

In our Western world, the most elaborate and definitive source of traditional knowledge about wisdom is contained in the Hebrew books of Proverbs and Wisdom. In Proverbs, the oldest book of the biblical wisdom literature, Lady Wisdom—"Hochma"—is referred to as a co-creator of the world with Jehovah himself. To her is ascribed an almost divine quality.

> Wisdom speaks her own praises, in the midst of her people she glories in herself.
>
> (Ben Sira 24:1–3, 9, 23)

And indeed she claims:

> Yahwe possessed me when his purpose first
> unfolded, before the oldest of his works.
> From everlasting I was firmly set,
> from the beginning, before earth came into being.
>
> (Prov. 8:22–24)

And she continues:

> I was by his side, a beloved little mother,
> delighting him day after day, ever at play

1 5 9

in his presence,
at play everywhere in his world
delighting to be with the sons of humanity.

(PROV. 8:29–31)

She exhorts her children gently, almost pleadingly:

Acquire Wisdom, acquire Perception,
never forget her, never deviate from my words.
Do not desert her, she will keep you safe,
love her, she will watch over you.

(PROV. 4:5–8)

When, however, they turn a deaf ear to her appeals, she
can also become exasperated and strident.

Does Wisdom not call meanwhile?
Does discernment not lift up her voice?
On the hilltop, on the road,
at the crossways, she takes her stand;
beside the gates of the city,
at the approaches to the gates she cries aloud,
O men! I am calling to you;
My cry goes out to the sons of humanity
You ignorant ones! Study discretion;
    and you fools, come to your senses!

(PROV. 8:1–6)

She can also be thoroughly feminine, endearingly court-
ing the sons of men.

She walks with him as a stranger,
and at first she puts him to the test;

1 6 0

Fear and dread she brings upon him
and tries him with her discipline;
With her precepts she puts him to the proof,
until his heart is fully with her.
Then she comes back to bring him happiness
and reveals her secrets to him.

(SIRACH 5:17–18)

Motherly care, however, a need to nourish her children, dominates when she prepares a feast and urges:

Come and eat my bread,
drink the wine I have prepared!
Leave your folly and you will live,
walk in the ways of perception.

(PROV. 9:12–16)*

For many people, I would presume, it is as surprising as it was for me to discover that "wisdom" in these ancient scriptures is represented as a woman existing since the beginning of time. She is, in fact, very much a woman, taking herself and her role proudly and seriously, yet delighting in the world and in "the sons of humanity." Her caring is as personal as that of a mother; her way of speaking straightforward, direct and simple. There is no demand for book knowledge, the cerebral, the cognitive, but rather a heartfelt cry for perception, paying attention with all the senses. Thoughts and feelings she expresses freely, and a deep need to nourish and care for humankind.

In further verses, she upbraids her sons for relentlessly

*Above quotes from Leonard Swidler, *Biblical Affirmations of Women.* Philadelphia: Westminster Press, 1979.

pursuing war and conquest and abandoning the skills of community living and peace.

With such a revered figure as Hochma championing their status, one might assume that women as depicted in the Hebrew scriptures were held in high regard. Many passages, however, describe them as being totally the property of their men. Service and obedience were, it would seem, their most highly prized virtues. Obviously this is what the patriarchal writers of the books wished to teach, and it does not depict the reality of daily life in any sensible way. The Jewish mother was surely always a powerful lady.

Let me introduce the figures of the two wise women of Takoa and Abel to support this statement. Their stories are told in 2 Samuel 14 and 20, respectively, representing early Israelite wisdom preceding the establishment of the kingship. These women held no official positions. They don't even have names. They do, however, speak with authority, using forms of language associated with prophecy and the wisdom tradition. Second class in status as women, they nevertheless challenged the judgments of two powerful men: the woman of Takoa that of the appointed ruler, David; the woman of Abel that of Joab, the leader of the Israelite forces. David refused to forgive and restore Absalom, his son and heir, from exile. The wise woman from Takoa successfully pleads for his return. The woman of Abel addressed Joab, calling to him from the walls of Abel, reminding him of its long-standing reputation as peaceful and faithful, "a mother in Israel." She then goes to the people in her city "in her wisdom" and they comply with her arbitration. The city is saved.

It is impossible not to assume that these women were powerful figures and customarily accorded authority within their own communities. Their approach to the tasks undertaken demonstrates previous experience in peaceful resolution of interpersonal disputes and community problems. Women who lived long enough would learn such adroitness in family affairs which in time would incorporate responsibility in a larger communal sphere.*

However, several women of the monarchic era following David are referred to in the scriptures as "wise women." A review of their stories reveals that they display few of the attributes of Lady Wisdom: perception, honesty, discretion, truth, and justice. Rather, their fame seems to be based on craftily plotted exploits which were finally highly advantageous for their men and resulted in the destruction of whatever enemy was threatening. Beauty, charm, and sometimes riches played a strong role in their success. Clever deception and bold action, seldom applauded as appropriate for women, are in these instances cited as laudable. Some of the names of these heroines we know well. We now praise their loyalty, valor, and courage. Perhaps such virtues were only appropriate in the service of the men and for what they all felt to be the survival of their people as well as the mythology of a patriarchal culture. Obviously, all the ordinary daily ordeals which women undertook to perform for the welfare of family and preservation of the race were never recorded in the annals of history or the sacred writings. Good women those, who accepted their blatantly inferior status in order to support the self-esteem of their men in the service of establishing a powerful nation. Hochma does not berate these wise women. It is the "sons of men" she addresses, reminding them, "I hate pride and arrogance," and urging that they "walk in the ways of perception." And sons of men are also sons of women. In

*Claudia V. Camp, "The Wise Women of 2 Samuel: A Role Model for Women in Early Israel?" *Catholic Biblical Quarterly*, Vol. 43 (January 1981), pp. 14–29.

this indirect way the men who wrote these passages are giving her an important claim on the future generations of the tribe of Israel as well as on the cultural heritage.

But let the wise Hebrew midwives of the Egyptian captivity be remembered, who, nonviolently and cleverly, resisted obeying the pharaoh's edict to kill the male children born to the Israelites. It was simply not possible to keep up with the task, they reported. The Hebrew women were too fecund.

This almost divine Lady Wisdom has her counterpart in Greek tradition—"Sophia," who lends her name to the great lovers of wisdom, the philosophers, and is lauded in the ancient writings. She shares the attributes of Hochma as the Stoic "Sophia." Later incorporated into the Christian tradition as "Aghia (Holy) Sophia," the great Greek orthodox basilica of Saint Sophia in Constantinople bears her name—this city which has such a long history of the coming together of so many sensory wonders both Oriental and Occidental.

Greece had its own goddess of wisdom, Athena, who originally came from Crete, where she was honored for her care of community living. Although worshipped for her attributes as guardian of fertility and goddess of wisdom, she also presided over the useful arts, especially pottery, weaving, and architecture. The Greek word was *technē* for art and *technikas* for craft, from which we derive *technology*. However, there is a "know-how" knowledge in the arts which places her connection with the arts (or rather the arts' vital connection to her as figurehead) with a type of knowledge, *technē*, which produces and creates from the senses and intuition. She had a strong following in the Mediterranean area and many temples existed in her honor.

When this "gray-eyed" goddess was adopted as

defender of Attica and Athens itself, she became a martial figure. The Olympian gods claimed her, giving her Zeus for a father, from whose head she was said to have sprung, fully armed.

Her symbol was the owl and her great shrine the Parthenon, a tribute to her almost forgotten but ardent advocacy of the arts, especially architecture and sculpture. Possibly in a patriarchal culture such as Greece became, it was only appropriate to worship this beloved goddess if she was fully armed and could thus embrace more manly skills. A city-state no longer needed a supreme mother earth goddess. There were frontiers to be guarded and expanded by an army and navy; the sea no longer offered adequate defense or boundaries.

There seems little doubt that these great ladies had for forebears the prevalent ancient mother goddesses of antiquity. In fact, everywhere in ancient thought, a principle which represents both wisdom and femininity can be discerned.

In an agricultural world, creativity, productivity, and procreativity were presided over by this dominant female principle. To live in community, creating all the necessities of practical life, placed major emphasis on the moral virtues, interrelationships and interdependence. Defense against attacks from outside invaders was no doubt important and called for manly, heroic valor. Ongoing, daily survival in community was, however, imperative and was entrusted to women. Wisdom in childrearing, in household matters, in herbal medicine, played an essential role in keeping struggling societies alive in the face of disease, illness, injury, and hunger. These threats were invaders of a different sort that had to be warded off at the threshold of each house. To fulfill all these requirements was an exhausting challenge but awarded little prestige, and certainly less than armed combat.

If we turn our attention to the Far East, we find similar

historical developments: the maternal order of the survival of the race displaced by the patriarchal order of technological progress and domination. In India the worship of the mother goddess is still strong and the evidence is pervasive that in various forms her worship was in ancient times dominant over the whole continent.* According to Vedic-Sanskritic tradition, and as acclaimed by the devotional hymns inspired by Hindu religiousness, the Devi, the great mother goddess, is primordial, present, and ultimate. She is a goddess of great power *(shakti):* Creative and destructive, immanent and transcendent, she presides as mother of the universe and daughter of the snowcapped Himalayas. But she is very present to human beings, since she is consciousness itself—consciousness as meaning the coordinated order of the senses. She is the cause of "what is bright."

Hindu sacred texts, however, offer us unequivocally a universe of paradox, and the great power of the Devi is expressed in her capacity to draw on all the obverse attributes of the benign qualities listed. She is glamorously beautiful, but can show herself as ugly and grotesque. Maternally compassionate, she, like a defending lioness, can also become a martial, all-powerful adversary.

Four great hymns to the Devi Mahatmya, dated from approximately a millenium and a half ago, extol her power and great virtues.

> To the great Goddess, by whom this world was stretched out through her own power, whose body is comprised of the powers of all the hosts of gods
> To Ambika, worthy of worship by all gods and great seers, are we bowed down with devotion; may she bring about auspicious things for us.

*Joan M. Erikson, *Mātā Nī Pachedi: The Temple Cloth of the Mother Goddess.* Ahmedabad, India: India Institute of Design, 1968.

During the heroic battle between the Asuras and the lower echelon gods, when the gods are beleaguered, they assemble on Mount Himavān and offer her a hymn:

Hail to the Goddess, hail eternally to the auspicious great Goddess!*

The hymn continues and in thirty-six verses praises her attributes. She is "the goddess who abides in all creatures" in the form of patience, modesty, contentment, and compassion, each virtue meriting its own verse and final "Hail, Hail!"

She is "the governess of the senses" in all creatures and is present in hunger, thirst, sleep, memory, tranquillity, as well as activity. And, most poetically, she is the goddess of "the inaccessible further shore."

The battle with the Asuras is won when she draws all the goddesses who represent certain aspects of her power back into *her own* form and thus becomes invincible. In iconography the goddess, Devi, is portrayed as standing on the head of a massive bull, one of the most mighty of the Asuras she has overpowered. Serenely poised she holds her trident and sword, bejeweled and beautiful.

But who are these Asuras and what was their offense? They appear to be the untamed sources of evil who constantly invade the civilized world, threatening to destroy its order. We may assume this to mean the social, earthly order by which human beings live, including the order of the senses—the loss of which could result in an exclusive preoccupation with domineering maleness. Callously such intruders may focus on holy places and desecrate them by destroying symbols and works of art,

---

*Both extracts, and textual quotes, from Thomas B. Coburn, *Devi Mahatmya*. Delhi: Motilal Banarsidas, 1984.

scoff at justice, disrupt tradition and teaching, and deni-
grate vision and values. Empathy, humility, and interre-
latedness can be derided. The male god figures,
accompanied by their Saktis, are the appointed protec-
tors of these supports and buttresses of community life
and order on earth. They usually manage successfully to
keep the Asuras in line and at bay. At the call of the gods
to her from Mount Himavān, the goddess does not destroy
the Asuras permanently, even when they are demolished
in battle. She only sends them back to their appropriate
place, a hell outside the god-governed world of humankind. They represent the dystonic and sometimes malign
elements in life which each individual must face and
subdue in order to develop staunch virtues and the higher
values of living in community.

With the introduction of Brahmanic literature, superior male gods, with female consorts *(shakti)* who are the
source of their vitality, became for the educated the focus
of worship and the source of wisdom. However, one story
about Shiva is memorable. He once spoke earnestly to
his sons, Ganesha and Kartikeya, expressing his wish that
they go out into the great, wide world and search for wisdom. Kartikeya took his spear and, mounted on his swift
peacock, set out to learn and achieve in distant parts.
Ganesha, the elephant-headed son, sat quietly for some
time, and then deliberately and thoughtfully began to walk
in a circle around his mother, Parvati, who was seated
nearby. Shiva was delighted and praised him for his
enlightened perception and understanding.

This beloved Ganesha, God of Wisdom and Lord of
Obstacles, whose ever-present *vahana* (vehicle or mount)
is a mouse, is encountered everywhere in the Far East.
He is worshipped in temples and in roadside and house-
hold shrines, not only in India but also in Cambodia, Java,
Nepal, and Tibet. The most cherished story about him,

which explains why he has only one whole tusk, is as follows:

As he rode home in the moonlight one night after feasting on a favorite Indian sweet, a cobra crossed his path and his mount reared and threw him to the ground. His round belly burst and the sweets were strewn around him. He refilled his belly and looked for something to hold him together. The cobra seemed to fill the need, so he used it as a belt. The moon had been watching this whole performance and burst out laughing. Ganesha was offended, broke off one tusk, and threw it at her, which extinguished her light. The nights all became dark and the gods begged him to relight the moon. So he finally did, but she still waxes and wanes and he is revenged.

Should we learn from this adventure that one does not laugh at the God of Wisdom even when he seems to be playing the fool? But Ganesha was not "playing the fool." He was alone on an empty, dark, country road. Thrown by his mount, he collected himself and what he scattered.

Using the snake, the cause of his accident, as a belt to pull himself together is a practical, sensible plan.

An empathic moon might have wiped a cloud from her face to give him better light. Instead she laughed at his expense and therefore his anger was justified.

Laughing at no laughing matter is an insult to wisdom.


The counterpart of the great Devi in Buddhism is Prajnaparamita—mother of all Buddhas. She is the Perfection of Wisdom, which emanates from her for the full enlightenment of all Buddhas. She provides guidance for all her sons in the world, and in this way takes her place side by side with the Buddha. The Prajnaparamita texts, with their emphasis on the feminine principle in the world, place her to some extent even above Buddha himself.

Nevertheless, the most often depicted Bodhisattvas, numbered among the highly revered emanations of the Buddha, are male divinities. A Bodhisattva is a supremely enlightened one who through many reincarnations compassionately seeks to lead all beings to Nirvana. Such a figure is Manjushri, who holds the transcendent wisdom of scripture in his left hand, and in his right hand bears "the flame-tipped, two-edged, razor-sharp sword of critical wisdom." To attain enlightenment, according to Buddha's teaching, requires great intellectual concentration. However, such concentration will be useless unless it goes hand-in-hand with the constant practice of active compassion. In Tibet the Bodhisattva of compassion is called Tara, "who helps us to 'cross' to the other shore, removes fear and dread, and grants the fulfillment of all our wishes." In China she is revered as Kuan Yin, "hearer of the cries of the world."* She has one thousand arms with which to hold the necessary remedies for her care of human beings.

As might be expected, the poorest elements of the population in China and in Tibet revere these Bodhisattvas of compassion most ardently, for their need is great. Village Indians, too, place their faith especially in the mother goddess, the Devi, in her various forms.

In South and Central America, also, the most adored and propitiated divinity is the Virgin Mother of God. Every town, village, and most households enshrine her image and invoke her sensed presence in daily life and her wise protection. In Europe and North America, she has her

---

*Quotes from Edward Conze, *Buddhism: Its Essence and Development*. New York: Harper Torchbooks, 1959.

adoring sons and daughters, for she reaches the heart directly through empathy without word or invocation.

Throughout the Western world the moral virtues have regularly been envisioned as female figures: Justice, Hope, Mercy, Liberty, Wisdom. One may indeed wonder why this is so when women are seldom if ever included in the councils of the powerful.

When we consider the awe and reverence which these ancient goddesses inspired, and their dominance the world over in the past, we are amazed that so little information about this fact appears in recorded history. At best, our knowledge of the past includes a patriarchal record of dynasties—the rise and fall of empires, trade routes, and conquests. Perhaps it is time to turn our attention to the maintenance and survival of Mother Earth, for which we need to revert to some ancient wisdom and skills.

But these words *reverence* and *awe* in the worship of caretaking gods lead us to consider what they mean to us and how they are related to wisdom.

## Awe, Wonder, and Reverence

### Awe

Many of us in the Western world have grown up aware of the severe edict "The fear of the Lord is the beginning of wisdom." For those who are persuaded that all personal attributes, including a final sense of wisdom, must follow a developmental pattern of growth, this is not acceptable. The word *fear* evokes a warning, stop sign, or a shrill danger signal demanding guilty compliance. Possibly "fear" is a mistranslation of Hebrew scripture. A preferable, more exact word may be *awe*, which, of course, can include an element of fear. Awe is associated with the sacred, the holy, or numinous, which, in the context of Hebrew scripture, does sound clearly appropriate.

Natural wonders are awe inspiring for many: a first impact with the quiet grandeur of the Grand Canyon, the thundering force of Niagara Falls, a majestic grove of ancient redwoods, Balboa's first glimpse of the Pacific when he thought he was in India. In this century technological invention and processes have (one after another) shattered all our preconceptions of the dimensions of time and space. This is especially so for elders, but the trip to the moon was surely experienced by many as both fearful and awesome.

All of these experiences demand attention, some perhaps evoking a quality of realistic apprehension in the presence of an overpoweringly awesome energy such as that in lightning, thunder, fire, and flood.

Such attention-commanding encounters are not all necessarily stimulated by natural events or technological achievements. Moments of breathtaking awe for which there are no adequate words may seem to stop time, exerting a weird fascination, enticing and extending into a rather formidable unknown.

To be on a hilltop with others witnessing an eclipse of the sun at midday is no doubt an awesome experience. To be quite alone, perhaps in the desert, for those long moments of darkness by day would bring close the awareness of the "mysterium tremendum" which holy persons and saints have tried to describe: somewhat akin to that awareness sought by our ancestors in the "spirit quest," which must be undertaken alone. Aloneness, then, heightens the sense of smallness, nakedness, and dependence to an unearthly degree—an experience sought for the soul's good, as young people the world over have always sensed.

William James, in *Varieties of Religious Experience,** reports the words of an informant as follows:

> For the moment nothing but an ineffable joy and exaltation remained. It is impossible fully to describe the experience. It was like the effect of some great orchestra, when all the separate notes have melted into one swelling harmony, that leaves the listener conscious of nothing save that his soul is being wafted upwards and almost bursting with its own emotion.

Using the analogy of an especially intense involvement in an art experience, these words describe a moment of almost religious wholeness. An element other than and beyond that which works of art "usually" arouse is here suggested. But art deals particularly with this borderline between transport and intense feeling evoking depths of both joy and sorrow, which are close to awe.

## Wonder

This gift of the experience of awe may mature through life or may be the lot of only a "special" few. However, it too must have early roots, which possibly can be nourished and supported throughout life. I suggest that its rudiments may be traced in the early years of life in the capacity to *wonder.*

Birth itself is, of course, always a miracle, and we are

*The Modern Library edition (Gifford Lectures). New York: Random House, 1902.

only now beginning to know something of the impact of this experience and the endurance of its effects on the development of the infant in subsequent life. In the first chapter of this book, the wonder expressed in that earliest instance of amazed perception that holds the infant for an intense moment of experiencing was described. A breathless moment of listening intently, of tasting with questioning surprise, of touching delicately may include such a look of wonder. The absorbed infant's first discovery that there are two sensitive antennae, two hands that can be controlled and reach for each other, is such a moment. Then in the breathlessness of that really magic moment when the earthbound crawler, quite spontaneously and unsupported, stands up alone and challenges gravity, both child and lucky observer are momentarily gripped by wondering appreciation of the innate purposefulness of growth.

Youngsters in the play ages bring us stories of wonder—fantasies and dreams. Shared experiences alert us to puzzling moments of wondering encounters.

A two-year-old boy stands at a wide-open window overlooking a valley. Suddenly bells ring out in the evening air. He looks startled and eagerly leans out, inquiring, "What's that?" "Those are bells ringing," is the answer offered. "Oh, where are they?" he asks excitedly. "They are way off in the distance," his mother says. "Oh, show me the distance, where is the distance?" The answer is unsatisfactory and troubling and he is quiet for a few minutes. Finally he compromises for the actual, the immediate: "Mommy, can we make some bells?"

A three-year-old comes running and excitedly shows us a tiny black spider with horny projections and clawlike legs. "Look, look," he says breathlessly, "I never saw a thing like that before in my *whole* life."

Everyday experiences with children which could be

multiplied *ad infinitum* teach us to stop, look, and wonder and, as we said earlier, to pay attention.

We are reminded of young Albert Einstein's fascinated response to the marvel of the compass, "Das ist ein Wunder." And we may have witnessed the marvel of the "diviner stick" which, when held by hand, equidistant at each end, for no apparent reason pulls one hand relentlessly and unfailingly toward the ground where water can be found. "Wonders will never cease" we were taught as children, and indeed we may only wish that the child's eye for and reverent acknowledgement of lesser wonders may never be dulled by prosaic acceptance as we age.

There are those individuals who experience a kind of exultation when finally their social role in life merges with a perception of available capacities and convictions: a merging of all life's threads into aspiration and purposefulness. Such a sense of self-affirmation may be totally realistic, even humble, but can be marked by a feeling of wonder-filled freedom and consolidation.

Half the songs of the world tell us of the wonder, the miracle of falling in love. God forbid that anyone should pass through life without this experience of deep joy. Slowly emerging love and long-lasting, warm relationships are a wonder to all witnesses who have realized fully the complexities of sustained mutuality.

The cycle of life itself, especially as elders consistently seek to integrate its many aspects, unfolds a supreme wonder. All sentient things come into being, integrate, develop, become, fulfill an appointed role, and die, to be returned to the earth. The whole earth, the planet, the cosmos, is in a state of constant change. We are all and with everything, involved in a process. Why? Faith, trust, and hope provide us with individual answers. We experience wonder, feel reverence, and apprehend awe, all prerequisites of wisdom. They force us to come to terms with our smallness in the vastness of the universe, the macrocosm and the microcosm in their wholeness. They merge with humility, the human inadequacy to grasp because of our not-knowingness, and evoke our need to revere experienced phenomena both seen and unseen in the distance and in the immediate present.

*Reverence*

It is as difficult to single out the observable vestiges of *reverence* in the early years of the life cycle as it is to recognize the moments when a sense of wonder is observable. Possibly this is so because such a moment is marked by an unusual quiet: a withdrawal, however short, into a space uninvaded by the noises and banalities of life. Even whispering seems inappropriate. An atmosphere or situation which commands quiet attention may evoke such a moment of reverence. A word, a sound, or a deep stillness; a sensitively appropriate gesture, a touch that has the quality of a blessing, the smell of incense or even burning leaves; perhaps the taste of a very special food or drink.

The eyeglasses and special personal effects of a saintly personage, like Gandhi, whom you then recognize as being also very human, may evoke such a withdrawal; the funeral of a young president or leader or death itself, which intrudes with its presence into both the mundane and the tension-promoting daily activities of living, may shock us into a state of reverence. To list even the most obvious potential stimuli would be an endless undertaking. However, a way of life that allowed a more reverential approach to all encounters, to all relationships, and to the materials and things of our existence might slow down what Rainer Maria Rilke described as "this slanting hour in which you see me hurry so," and help us to "come to our senses," as Lady Hochma adjures.

## Attributes of Wisdom

*Wisdom* remains an elusive word because it encompasses an attitude, a disposition toward life, past, present, and future, only occasionally recognized in rare individuals. But through the ages people have come to look for it in the ways and words of old men and women marking the caliber of the strengths gained from decades of living.

When we do encounter wisdom in an old person, we find that it has little to do with sages and wise men and knowledgeable great minds. Vast book knowledge as such is not a requirement—but a richness of experience *is* a potential generator of wisdom, a recognition through the senses of the richness and diversity of life which on the surface might seem to have been an uneventful one.

Indeed, where does one look for a listing of all the attributes of wisdom? Some elements are so undebatable that we can nominate them without hesitation. If we are to understand the development of these virtues we may also determine where in the life cycle, as we have described it, each one has its roots. Attributes develop slowly and though they may be present in vestigial form, even in the genes, they manifest themselves epigenetically over time. Since wisdom is the strength which reaches full fruition only in old age, it must therefore be an all-pervasive goal of every stage of life. Ten character strengths appear to be inclusive of all the others which might claim listing as attributes of wisdom.

### Interdependence and Interrelatedness

The word *dependence* is derived from the Latin *pendere*—to hang, as a pendant hangs down from a necklace. *Depend* is used only in connection with other forms such as "on someone or something" for aid and support. However, it also has the very positive meaning "to rely on or place trust in someone or something." Early in childhood one begins to learn the reciprocity involved in dependence because it is necessary to the development of dependability. Learning to trust in our own capacities as well as in those of others also implies a responsive trustworthy reliability.

In old age when disability becomes part of ongoing experiences, the elder or invalid again must adapt to an appropriate dependence. The word *appropriate* cannot be underscored heavily enough since mistrust of available support is maladaptive and an excessive dependence leads to inactivity and withdrawal. Trust in mutuality and in the accurately perceived dependability of the senses marks the presence of sturdy roots of wisdom. The wise elder has learned to understand *interdependence*, the ecology of living with others. Early training and much of adult life stress independence, which if pressed to absurdity leads one to isolation and emotional stagnation. Human beings need one another, and their vital involvement in relationships nourishes and sustains the whole cycle of life. This is the law of the natural world. The acceptance of it as a fundamental precept can dispose us to find our places, as it were, organically on this planet.

But where and when does this sense of oneness with others and even with inanimate matter originate in the life cycle? How do the essential rudiments of a sense of *interdependence* develop? We would propose that the earliest experiences of mutuality with the caring persons and the matrix itself offer the infant the trust in the senses and in *dependent* relationships which can be sustained and augmented throughout the life cycle. Where this trusting dependence is never evoked or remains utterly inadequate the infant withdraws into apathy and does not survive. As we have already stressed, every living person, therefore, has this basic capacity to varying degrees, which can be further supported by positive experiences of mutuality throughout life.

### Acceptance of the Cycle of Life from Integration to Disintegration

The word *integration* describes the organization of constituent elements into a coordinated whole. Developmentally this would imply continued growth into an integral maturity followed by slow *disintegration* into old age and death. The acceptance and affirmation of epigenetic growth in childhood and youth with consistent, stagewise development of appropriate ego strength are the challenge of integration. Here the wisdom of the senses, first learned by the actively curious, exploring youngster as experiential knowledge about the body and its capacities and about the surrounding materials of the environment with their laws and properties, becomes enduringly trustworthy.

In later life a slow loss of physical and sensory capacities must also be appropriately perceived, accepted, and affirmed. The word again to be stressed is *appropriate*, for in early years overstimulus and inhibition are both maladaptive. In old age a passive acceptance of a stereotype which limits and stagnates induces apathy and withdrawal. Although a medium of disintegration must consistently be faced, it can be modified by equally consistent integrative procedures. One senses in the wise old men and women of the world that they have accepted aging and death as beyond human resolution and indeed as the nature of sentient things. They have learned to incorporate the unknown as if it were familiar—more familiar than any "known" truth. In fact, to suppose one is, or should be, an exception is blatant presumption.

## Resilience

*Resilience* "is the power to spring back or return to an original form after being compressed, bent, or stretched." It is used also to describe a recovery from illness, depression, or any other adversity. Every morning brings the challenge to exert our resiliency for we know well that each day brings surprise and change, losses and gains. Gains are usually somewhat easier to accept with equanimity than losses, which cause despair since a great longing exists both to have and to hold.

At the play stage, children play out this loss and gain repeatedly with "hide-and-seek," "cops and robbers," "treasure hunts," and innumerable other inventive games. They are also devastated by the loss of a beloved toy, animal, or person. Resiliency is practiced in their play life, and this is a great good since the need for this attribute remains constant throughout life.

Perhaps we err when we applaud early virtuosity in school and encourage specialization, which restricts later choices. Closing too many doors early in life may make resilience more difficult when times and capacities change. In any case, throughout life resilience is mandatory in a changing world, and never more so than in that last stage when one may have thought that calm sameness would prevail.

*Empathy*

The word *empathy* comes to us from the Greek *empatheia*, meaning "affection." Perhaps it is only possible to experience vicariously the feelings or attitudes of another when at least a modicum of affection exists. Even to identify with another person, animal, or object must demand a knowing which is only possible where a sense of the other has been perceived and absorbed, as, for example, confirmed by the infant's facial expressiveness in response to the mother's animated attention. Certainly this begins very early in life and becomes a central issue in the play of the young preschool child. Taking turns in games, playing roles—fireman, policewoman, nurse, and grocer—and preoccupation with imaginative stories highlight play hours. A rich experience of such play is fertile ground for the development of interrelationship and the rudimentary lessons of understanding, and thus of empathizing with others.

Life also teaches us that only the wisdom which involves a deep and honest knowledge of ourselves makes possible the most empathic of all statements: "There but for the grace of God go I." Every possible calamity might have been our lot: All the sicknesses, weaknesses, and perversions which assail human beings we are also prone to, and have in some measure tasted and recognized in ourselves. Where such empathy exists the quoted phrase might more aptly read "There *because* of the grace of God go I,"* for such mutuality is indeed a grace and empowers understanding, forgiveness, and humility. True wisdom and empathy affirm our vulnerability and evoke our acceptance of this knowledge with gratitude.

*A revision suggested by Dr. Otto Will in a group conversation.

There is no stage of our interwoven life with others which does not demand this attribute in quantity and quality. An old age which does not involve a constant reminiscing about friends and acquaintances past and present with perceptive empathy could be dull and cold. How else can a life lived be recollected except as stimulated by the presence of the vital young, who re-evoke past experiences and recall past relationships. Empathy, which is a powerful bond, may, in fact, be that force in life which counteracts what scientists designate as "all-pervading entropy": that energy which consistently spreads out and disassociates all matter.

*Humor*

However, this attribute must go hand-in-hand with the capacity to distinguish fantasy from reality so that a strong sense of purposefulness maintains the boundaries of playfulness and actuality. The tension of this demand is alleviated by the playing child's refreshing sense of *humor*—healing, enlivening laughter that keeps human feet firmly on the ground *(humus)*. The world being full of incongruities, perplexity would surely be overwhelming if humor abandoned us. Who has not heard with relish how children giggle at the absurd things they see, and the falseness of telephone voices they often hear? To turn things around or upside down is the imagination's way of maintaining a perspective on the pro forma irrationalities of social conformity. When we can see even ourselves as funny, it eases this daily living in such close proximity with ourselves.

It does have its negative counterpart, however. Intellectual wit with its sharp, clever observations can be both aggressive and mean, a weapon rather than a healer. In the aging it is apt to take the form of disdain, and can be both isolating and chilling.

*Resiliency, empathy,* and *humor* are, as described, all firmly rooted and nourished in the play life of children before schooling begins. This should give us pause when we learn that play school and kindergarten are now being invaded by those who would encourage the teaching of math, reading, and computer science, in order to give children an early start in schooling. Such overzealous commitment to cognitive skills may well be a great misfortune.

*Humility*

Perhaps empathy and humor lead our way into humbleness since throughout the ages wisdom has been associated with respect for genuine *humility* (an attribute not to be confused with conspicuous humility, which is suspect). Its opposite—arrogance—distances, forming barriers and suggesting elitism. Humility allows us awareness of incapacities and with that also a coolly accurate assessment of our own physical, cognitive, and aesthetic competencies. It is also a property of teachability for both young and old, and therefore a prerequisite for learning throughout life. Inappropriate overassessment of an ability or capacity is not likely if it is accurately perceived and judged. This provides a realistic measure of how clearly one's perception "says true," especially about oneself. When this competence is developed with true humility, how greatly it can free and enhance one's appreciation of the vastness of excellence which one perceives in others, in the cultural store of the great works of literature, and in all great achievements of art.

## A Sense of the Complexity of Living

The wisdom that may accrue with age will necessarily be marked by a *sense of the complexity of living*, of relationships, of all negotiations. There is certainly no immediate, discernible, and absolute right and wrong, just as light and dark are separated by innumerable shadings. Justice is not the province of a computer. Historical relativity completely changes the meaning of an event and a chance relativity of position distorts perception. This interweaving of time and space, light and dark, and the complexity of human nature suggests that to understand a situation in its contextuality is in truth superhuman. In life it can be only roughly approximated—a degree of wisdom which perhaps only Solomon ever attained.

This wholeness of perception, if it is to be even partially realized, must of necessity be made up of a *merging* of the *sensual*, the *logical*, and the *aesthetic* perceptions of the individual. The senses are the antennae, the trusted informants of our physical being, and have been so since infancy. They must, however, be trustworthy and maintained in their trustworthiness even when one has learned and continues to learn their limitations. Cognition is valid only when tested by experience. The aesthetic sense is in its essence the perception of the oneness of all manifested matter.

We come at this stage, also, to begin to sense an existential identity, the core of which we first became aware when, at some early age, we realized that we were not part of anyone else—that we were alone. It probably never leaves us, although some feel it more as a consistent estrangement, while others become, perhaps purposely, more deeply involved in the social matrix in which they live. In adolescence and young adulthood the tension of deciding what one's psychosocial identity is to be becomes focal and often all consuming. This involves choosing a work role and preparing for it. To that will be added a chosen family role and also a role in the community. These roles can be and are "played" experientially with genuine involvement, and this play provides a contextuality in working through complexity. However, in late adolescence or young adulthood, a consistent sense and awareness of an invariant core, the essence of one's self, which is the steady onlooker and consistent defender of the existential identity, the "I" of one's being, can begin to become firm.

### Recognition of the Complexity of Sustained Relationships

In mature intimacy, with its commitment to responsibility for another person or several others, the adult learns to cope with the extraordinary *complexity of sustained relationships.* The mutuality required, we believe, is the source of a true understanding of human relationships and, indeed, makes possible a grasp of the demanding complexity of living in community. However, interdependent life also demands of mutuality the alternate mode of *solitariness,* which provides a maintained balance between both social involvements and the individual's need to support the developmental needs of the personal "I."

### Caritas

Caring for and about things, people, and the world itself, we have claimed, is the virtue, the strength of the seventh stage, adulthood. In elders these commitments maintain and are a major form of their vital involvement with the matrix in which they live. This commitment keeps them needed and included, and without these involvements a sense of detachment can tend to isolate.

There is, however, an attribute of wisdom that seems of great importance which can be described as nonpossessive attachment. It is possible to care for and about things, and of course individuals as well as this green earth, without dominating anything. "Let it be," the song repeats. "Let it be."

The wise old man or woman learns to go lightly, receive gratefully, release easily, in order to feel as unfettered as possible. Loss is inevitable, so holding on is defeating. Resignation is regrettable, but an active freeing and emptying is a creative option.

## Existential Identity

With the final stage of aging, now so much longer for the many than it ever was before, comes the time for consistent integration to offset the impact of loss and physical disintegration. Constant change encourages apathy and remoteness and presents formidable challenges: Despair seems natural. But presumably, values have become staunch and integral and hope is part of acceptance; the time is ripe for an integration of past, present, and future into the final *existential identity*. Such an identity transcends the self and underscores the presence of intergenerational links.

An existential identity must meaningfully contain, but not be limited by, the psychosocial identity. Based on all the strengths and insights which have emerged from the stages of life as lived in one's historical moment, it reaches out to encompass an identity which is universal in its acceptance of the human condition.

We look for these indices, these traits, in people, especially in old people. We figure they have had more time, more experience to develop, in particular, that inner core which is invariant and balances out life's incongruities. We find it in surprising instances, perhaps especially where it has been honed by vital experiences, unencumbered by any conscious effort to be wise: simply to live fully and meaningfully—for and with others.

When we consider each of the attributes of wisdom we have listed and their place in life-cycle development, it would be impossible to state that these are predominantly feminine or masculine values. They are essential for men, who, however, have elected to underscore courage, valor, and achievement as particularly manly values.

This reminds me of a story which first amused us but then became very meaningful. In the fifties when we worked in Stockbridge, we attended a lecture presented by Margaret Mead to a small audience of psychiatrists and guests. Her topic was the role of the postmenopausal red-tailed deer which, she said, had been observed in the far north. In their old age, when all the old bucks had been killed off in contentious fighting over priorities and in territorial skirmishes, the females became the oldest survivors. In time of drought, these old does could remember where once long ago under similar circumstances water sources had been found. When spring came late, they recalled sunny slopes where the snows melted early. They knew how to find sheltered places where blizzards could be waited out. Under such circumstances, they took over the leadership of the herd. Old age, she postulated, has a unique contribution to make when well-stored, long experience and practical know-how, fortitude, and hope are required. Women throughout time have practiced and nurtured these skills for

community living, and they serve ongoing species survival.

The martial values which men have emulated and
claimed as obviously necessary for purposes of attack and
defense are becoming obsolete in our push-button era.
Men have, over the last centuries, added to their dominance of the martial skills a supremacy in the cognitive
and scientific enterprise and claimed these also as their
particular areas of expertise. Now that women have begun
to demonstrate their capacities as philosophers, scientists, and financiers, such a dichotomy is no longer ten-
able. Probably we should be reasonable and sensible, and
designate all the attributes of wisdom as necessary and
universal age-old survival skills.

## The Fool, the Jester, and the Artist

Having listed these attributes of wisdom, which sometimes seem to be exemplified in old men and women, is
it feasible also to specify how life must be lived in order
to support their development? There are certainly many
ways that may be chosen and followed, but I will present
and defend the way of the fool, the jester, and the artist.

First, it is important to deal with various meanings of
the word *fool,* for I shall speak of a chosen way, not one
unalterably defined by genes. Natural fools have existed
in society, one must assume, since time immemorial—
those variously slow-witted ones who could be cherished
and protected in small communities as "children of God"
even in adulthood.

In medieval times a special and lively role was available for the playful, witty entertainer who could evoke
laughter and join the troubadours on the great pilgrim-

ages which were then so popular. A pilgrimage was a severe test of courage and stamina, much like life's long, arduous journey, and the fool has had and often still enjoys privilege and support for his very presence. His impudence and disrespect for the accepted social order were tolerated possibly as a respite from the seriousness of the quest. Some of his immunities have long been shared by itinerant actors, mimes, gypsies, and even hoboes and beachcombers. Such "fools" become an expression of the teasing and rebellious urges in human beings, which society undertakes to suppress. They earn our envy in part because of their stubborn refusal to accept the strictures of convention, thus making themselves in many ways free.

All through the Middle Ages, also, saints and wise men and women who lived their lives teaching and preaching were revered as "fools of God." Wandering penniless they claimed no home and begged for their food in the name of God and charity. Such a figure was Francis of Assisi, who was later canonized. Jacopone da Todi, one of his many followers, carried on his tradition singing laudi where he traveled, writing and reciting poems and dramatizing his message with conspicuous poverty and humility. Often such "holy fools," as they provided interplay between the arts, wisdom, and foolishness, acquired an awesome prestige and honor.

Another role became important in Elizabethan times, that of the very privileged court jester. An actor and, no doubt, a facile mimic, song, dance, humor, and even wit were the tools of trade with which he eased his master's tensions and lightened a king's responsibilities. Completely dependent on his lord and beholden to no one else, he was nevertheless free to be entirely himself and was given free rein in his master's service. Perceptive, resilient to all moods, he teasingly guided with his clowning, and this with courage and the wisdom of uncluttered vision.

In Shakespeare's tale of King Lear we see this fool portrayed with a display of real wisdom combined with extravagant foolishness. This powerful old king decides in a moment of utter foolish and petulant vanity to give away his whole kingdom to his flatterers. Few of the courtiers dare press the angry king to change his decision. The jester, however, can allow himself to say:

> FOOL. If thou wert my fool, nuncle I'd have thee beaten for being old before they time.
> LEAR. How's that?
> FOOL. Thou shouldst not have been old 'til thou hadst been wise.

This is audacious, indeed, but he carried it off with humor and finally, with single-minded devotion, follows his lord into exile. In the end Lear comes to his senses and is reunited with his other faithful fool, Cordelia.

To be sure, Lear's fool is an idealized version of a jester's identity and life, but it serves to underscore some of the demands made on him as well as his great privileges. To evoke gaiety and the release of laughter in a court setting was no small challenge. Indeed, the laughing applause acknowledged and celebrated the relationship of the courtiers to his and their own foolishness. Success was a high moment, one imagines; failure only brought scorn or a cuffed ear.

If we seek out those who evoke some of this kind of applause in our modern world, we find the entertainer, the humorist, the comic. Some reach the pinnacle of success, and in various ways make us all laugh. Others, perhaps less witty or lucky, or for whom the historical moment is not yet ripe, are unable to live "by their wits" and talents. Young people often are called foolish because they wish to pursue a path which to society seems impractical.

A young college student who was not doing well with his studies went to a center where it seemed possible that he might "get straightened out." He worked with a therapist, but also in a shop where creative activities were possible under the aegis of artists. He became a very capable and devoted potter. He also became consolidated in other ways and prepared to leave the center. On telling his parents, both professionals, that he planned to work with clay and become a potter, they were dumbfounded. "A potter . . .? But you can't make a living being a potter. And how about college?" The rest of this particular story is not pertinent.

A young woman halfway through college announces that she intends to become a dancer. Her shocked parents respond, "That's impossible—that's foolhardy." Others agree with them, and that is just and correct, for such a fool must indeed be very hardy—and determined.

Cultures other than our own have quite another attitude toward the arts, especially painting, sculpture, music, and architecture. They generously support these arts and hold artists in high regard. Recently the line between these fine arts and the lower echelon arts, such as ceramics, textiles, glassblowing, metalworking, and etching, has become more than blurred, since many renowned artists have begun to work with these other materials. In our country, however, not even acclaimed artists can financially join the ranks of pensioned professionals in other more practical fields.

Parents respond to this knowledge but have little understanding of the quality and satisfaction of the life of an artist—of its autonomy and rich association with other creative individuals.

The way to "success" in the arts is a pyramid watched over by a sphinx, and she never predicts who will make it to the top for immediate success or for long-range acclaim. Immediate notoriety is such a question of promotion and / or a merging with fashionable trends, as well as the historical moment, that it defies prediction. The great artists whom we now speak of with reverence, many of whom died in poverty and were neglected in their time, lived lives consecrated to their work. Yet one can believe they had a sense of fulfillment which was for them right and true.

Artists—creative people whose lives are attuned to their work—seem to live in a world they are constantly discovering and delighting in, with song, dance, and laughter, in the beauty around them, and the uniqueness of relationships. One might say of them what Rilke wrote of Orpheus: "Praising was all—praising was his mission."

These are individuals who know they have a calling, a deep urgency to work with materials, with sound, with dance, drama, or poetry. This overriding need sustains them and gives them the courage to proceed, regardless of the values of the many who surround them. In a chosen way, like that of the jester or the fool, the experience of and dedication to creativity (art and Art) become their overlord and give them license to be free, to be themselves.

This portrait of the artist is as "idealized" as that of the fool presented earlier. What artist can we point to, past or present, of such single-minded integrity? Yet enough exemplify these characteristics to permit a composite presentation. The dedication of many, the great as well as the less known, is a constant inspiration.

This "artist's way" demands a commitment to be undertaken only if genuine conviction supports the necessary stamina. To live fully in the present moment rather

I argue that some artists get their creativity from unhappiness than striving for some future satisfaction runs contrary to our social norms. Paying consistent attention with sensitivity to the materials and processes of creative activity demands involvement. This is rewarded by a constant discovery of the less-known properties and potentials of materials and provides immediate satisfaction, generating further impetus and experimentation. An ongoing reaching out for genuine, deeper universal expression, while maintaining a personal uniqueness and integrity, leads the artist on. This search for the essence of the material incorporated in the process and in the art form is a lifelong quest. The "I" of the artist, the invariant core of his or her being, is challenged wholly and consistently.

The artist shares this all-or-nothing stance with the "fool of God." Both can "do no other." Their ways sometimes merge, as demonstrated by Saint Francis, who was indeed an artist and a saint. They do not preclude each other, but, on the contrary, are alike in their single-mindedness. For the artist also would find the way drab and repellent without song, humor, dance, drama, and an intimate relationship between body, senses, and the beautiful.

There are, however, other similarities shared by the artist, the fool, and the jester which I would like to underscore. All have the capacity to bind the past, present, and future and remain unfettered by today's clock or schedule. Most of us live in a time span which dictates an image of behavior and ideals of success toward which we strive both consciously and unconsciously. The fool and the artist to a greater or lesser degree live outside this time-space frame, and have played their respective roles throughout history and everywhere in the world. Related to the shaman and oracles in "primitive" times, artists played their parts in the ordered collective with music, dance, incantation, and the graphic arts. Their place was an honored one and we are enriched by tracing their footprints. They have always been with us.

In their ways of living and being they draw out of all of us a response to our own playfully expressive and inventive past, which we look back on with nostalgia and wonder. We try to recapture this childhood today as we seek out recreation to escape from our ordered, time-bound lives, but too often we fail to retrieve the magic. The fool and the artist are capable of living with a sense of surprise and anticipation which seems to promise an enlivened and enticing future. Their lives and their creations make us hopeful even in a world pregnant with bad omens.

The artist is also less inclined to pattern his or her living or working space along the lines of social norms—and claims this freedom. His or her chosen space allows flexibility—elbow room in which to realize fantasies, intuitions, images; to give them possible form, appraise and play with the potentials of materials and processes. It is an inner space, stimulating the senses, inviting ideas as well as the making and doing activities of the arts. It is intimate without necessarily being small, allowing a freedom from the intrusions of outer space and its demands.

Now let me say that I am convinced that all of us have something of the fool in us which keeps us human and sometimes wise. We are all much more creative than we realize. Many more people are learning to allow themselves to be different, to be themselves, and to tolerate the "differences" of others. We applaud individuality in the way people plan the space in which they prefer to live, and the idiosyncratic management of their lives.

194

For many, television has brought about the sad loss of our capacities to entertain ourselves with singing, dancing, storytelling, and games. Television is sedentary and often lonely, whereas group recreation is interpersonal and enlivening. Perhaps we can re-create these good things in new ways. When we are free of social dictates that are unnecessarily restricting, we can be resilient. I salute the fool in all of us.

Why not envision a renaissance in which art and its language are generally understood and truly universal; where in childhood creativity is promoted, given scope, and nourished in such a way that it remains a firm substructure of adult lives?

History could then be studied, not by means of the written records of conquests and battles, but by what people at any given time created and venerated. We are beginning to do this, and it is astonishing how we flock to museums to learn to know and appreciate the artwork of other peoples. To our great enrichment the writings of the poets of other lands are also now being translated as never before. Any belittling of foreign regions such as we have previously indulged in is impossible when we see, hear, and respect their great artistic accomplishments. Many of us are also searching out and reclaiming our "foreign" ancestral roots with new interest in our forebears in this new world.

This bonding of the peoples of the world through acknowledgement of the universality of human reverence for beauty and its truth could support our sense of oneness and interdependence. Our own bonding to the past should deepen an appreciation of our creative potentials and reinforce a hope for a future of conservation, creativity, and enlightened justice.

Is this a wild flight of fantasy? Yes, but so also was the

dream that launched Columbus on his trip to India, followed by others, in search of a space in which to create a whole new world.

But let me end on a lighter vein. Earlier I wrote of Ganesha, the Indian god of wisdom, and his relationship with his mother, Parvati. As the story indicates, his sense of wisdom, he believed, had been generated by this mother.

One day Parvati, wishing to bathe, asked Ganesha to guard her premises. As he did so, Shiva arrived and demanded to join her in the bathing area. Ganesha insisted on guarding his mother's privacy and Shiva in a fury cut off his head. Parvati immediately appeared and angrily reminded her husband that this was their son, and Shiva rushed off to find another head for Ganesha. An elephant was first to come his way, and he immediately severed its head, brought it back, and placed it on Ganesha's headless body.

Ganesha is much beloved in India and taken very seriously by everyone, including himself, which he demonstrates by his sense-centered ways. As the Lord of All Obstacles, he is never defeated by apparent impossibilities. He is therefore invoked at the beginning of all enterprises, and the stories of how he achieves his purposes are full of surprises and a generous gaiety. With short arms and legs and a ponderous belly, he seems full of a gentle inner joy. Sometimes depicted as dancing with delight, he proceeds in a leisurely fashion, not at all in the spirited, ecstatic way of his great father.

That he is always shown in painting and sculpture with his mount, a mouse, is a not-too-subtle joke, again demonstrating the Indian delight in and respect for paradox.

## Wisdom

Is this story telling us that wisdom may not be taken by assault, and is a private treasure, well guarded? We do well to recall Hochma's plea:

> She walks with him as a stranger
> and at first she puts him to the test;
> Fear and dread she brings upon him
> And tries him with her discipline;
> With her precepts she puts him to the proof,
> Until his heart is fully with her.
> Then she comes back to bring him happiness
> And reveals her secrets to him.

Wisdom, which most of us have taken to be such an exalted achievement found only in hoary old age, appears to have its feet firmly on the ground, *humus*, which is also *mundus* (mundane), both of which are those close relatives of humor. They point only to a creative way that perhaps enables the making of "a silken purse out of a sow's ear," or out of whatever material life sends your way.

But the poet, artist, maker shall have the last word.*


## To Orpheus

As once the winged energy of delight
carried you over childhood's dark abysses,
now beyond your own life build the great
arch of unimagined bridges.

*From Stephen Mitchell, trans. and ed., *The Selected Poetry of Rainer Maria Rilke*, © 1982 by Stephen Mitchell. Reprinted by permission of Random House, Inc.

Wonders happen if we can succeed
in passing through the harshest danger;
but only in a bright and purely granted
achievement can we realize the wonder.

To work *with* Things in the indescribable
relationship is not too hard for us;
the pattern grows more intricate and subtle,
and being swept along is not enough.

Take your practiced powers and stretch them out
until they span the chasm between two
contradictions . . . For the god
wants to know himself in you.

# Index

# INDEX

Schoenbrun, Mary, 79
school age, 92–95, 130
  artistic expression in, 93–94
  competence in, 78, 86, 92–95, 119–20
  discipline in, 93, 120
  distonic polarity of, 119–20
  inertia and, 119, 120
  materials and, 95
  modern social order and, 93–94, 119–20
  narrow virtuosity and, 119, 180
  resilience in, 120, 180
  sensory development in, 26, 30–32, 35, 36
  skills developed in, 92–93
  syntonic vs. distonic polarities and, 78, 92–95, 119–20
schools, 13, 25, 120, 132
  art programs in, 94–95
  creative activities in, 50
  play age in, 33–34, 91–92, 183
  sensory development and, 26, 30–35, 36
Schopenhauer, Arthur, 113
science, 49–50, 75
sculptors, 13, 46, 54, 132
*Selected Poetry of Rainer Maria Rilke, The* (Mitchell, trans. and ed.), 197n
senses, development of, 11–12, 14, 17–45, 66, 75, 104, 111, 132
  adulthood and, 29–30, 39–41
  appropriate stimuli needed in, 24–25, 39, 82
  arts and, 26, 36, 42, 44
  attention in, 37–38, 41
  creative activities in, 42, 44, 45, 50
  early childhood and, 22–23, 27–29, 33–34, 36, 38
  eating habits in, 39–40
  epigenesis of, 24
  experiential knowledge in, 23, 25–26, 32, 33–34, 36, 48, 49, 179
  fetuses and, 18–19, 20, 21, 24, 69, 74–75, 79, 81, 87
  genetic differences in, 24, 79, 93
  giftedness and, 13, 24, 30, 32–33
  hazards to, 39–41
  hearing in, 18, 21, 24, 25, 35, 39, 55, 83
  human potentials and, 17–18
  imagination and, 35–36
  infancy and, 18, 19–22, 24, 29, 38, 40, 81, 82, 83, 85, 87, 115
  kinesthetic sense in, 24–25, 43–44, 84–85, 88–89, 109
  memory in, 35–36, 41–44, 158

modern social order and, 22–23, 25, 35, 36, 39–41
old age and, 42–45
play age and, 23, 27–29, 30, 33–34
school age and, 26, 30–32, 35, 36
schools in, 26, 30–35, 36
sense organs in, 18, 21–22, 24–25, 39–41, 83
sensory impairment and, 24, 36–37, 39–40, 83
smell in, 19, 21, 24, 25, 40, 85
survival dependent on, 26, 111
taste in, 18, 19, 21, 24, 25, 39–40
touch in, 21–22, 24, 25, 35, 40–41, 83, 87
vision in, 19, 22, 24, 25, 35, 39, 55, 83
wisdom and, 156, 166, 167, 184
wonder in, 26–30
Shakespeare, William, 13, 103, 190
*Shakespeare's Game* (Gibson), 134
*shakti*, 166, 168
shamans, 193
shame and doubt, autonomy vs., 78, 79, 84–85, 88–90, 97, 102, 109, 116–18, 121, 128, 130
Shiva, 46, 168, 196
sin, 118
Sirach, 160–61, 197
skin, 21–22, 35, 40, 87
smell, sense of, 19, 21, 24, 25, 40, 85
*Social Life in Britain from the Conquest to the Reformation* (Coulton), 133n
social order, modern, 75, 101, 125
  creative activities in, 49–50, 53, 55, 65
  early childhood and, 22–23, 48–49, 89, 116–17
  school age and, 93–94, 119–20
  schools and, 13, 120
  sensory development and, 22–23, 25, 35, 36, 39–41
  technology in, 13, 50, 75, 119, 164, 166, 172
  television in, 39, 55, 93, 195
  wisdom in, 156–59, 188, 195
Socrates, 29
"Some Reflections on Dolls" (Rilke), 54n, 55n, 56n, 57n
Sophia, 164
space, 122, 172, 193
  body, 69–70
  creative activities and, 51–52, 68–70
  form and, 68–70
  limitations of, 70
  living, 51–52, 95, 135, 194
stagnation, generativity vs., 47, 78, 87, 99–103, 105–6, 123–24, 132, 133